The

SOCRATIC
DIALOGUES

The

SOCRATIC DIALOGUES

PLATO
FOREWORD BY MORRIS KAPLAN, PH.D.
TRANSLATION BY BENJAMIN JOWETT

PUBLISHING

New York

This publication is designed to provide accurate and authoritative information in regard to the subject matter covered. It is sold with the understanding that the publisher is not engaged in rendering legal, accounting, or other professional service. If legal advice or other expert assistance is required, the services of a competent professional should be sought.

Foreword © 2008 by Morris Kaplan, Ph.D.

© 2009 by Kaplan, Inc.

Published by Kaplan Publishing, a division of Kaplan, Inc.
1 Liberty Plaza, 24th Floor
New York, NY 10006

All rights reserved. The text of this publication, or any part thereof, may not be reproduced in any manner whatsoever without written permission from the publisher.

Printed in the United States of America

Library of Congress Cataloging-in-Publication Data

Plato.
 [Dialogues. English. Selections]
 The Socratic dialogues / Plato ; foreword by Morris Kaplan ; translation by Benjamin Jowett.
   p. cm.
 ISBN 978-1-4277-9953-1 (pbk.)
 1. Philosophy. I. Kaplan, Morris, Ph. D. II. Jowett, Benjamin, 1817-1893. III. Title.
 B358.J82 2009
 184--dc22
                          2008035882

10 9 8 7 6 5 4 3 2 1

ISBN-13: 978-1-4277-9953-1

Kaplan Publishing books are available at special quantity discounts to use for sales promotions, employee premiums, or educational purposes. Please email our Special Sales Department to order or for more information at kaplanpublishing@kaplan.com, or write to Kaplan Publishing, 1 Liberty Plaza, 24th Floor, New York, NY 10006.

CONTENTS

Socratic Method?
by Morris Kaplan, Ph.D. vii

Euthyphro 1

Apology 31

Crito 63

Lysis 83

Laches 119

Charmides 161

Preview of Morris B. Kaplan's Introduction to Xenophon's
Memorable Thoughts of Socrates 201

SOCRATIC METHOD?

Morris B. Kaplan
Professor of Philosophy
Purchase College SUNY

Among the tactics creating "shock and awe" for first-year law students around the country is their first encounter with "Socratic method." This phrase describes the rigorous interrogation that their teachers use to force them to explain and apply authoritative legal decisions to changing patterns of fact. Their ability to remain consistent and coherent is tested in the face of contradictory or confusing conclusions. It sometimes comes as a surprise to learn that the man whose name is assigned to this process was no lawyer or judge but rather a "philosopher." Not only that, but his major encounter with the law resulted in his conviction of major crimes. The historical Socrates lived in Athens all of his life, fought in its army during the war against Sparta, and faced capital charges in his native city. In 399 BCE, he was found guilty of "impiety" and "corrupting the youth." Sentenced to death, he famously refused an offer of escape arranged by his friends and was duly executed at the age of 70. Socrates left no writings by which later generations could determine what he thought. What did he teach? What got him into such trouble? How can we know? Why does it matter?

Socrates's status as a founder of Western philosophy results from the work of his student and friend Plato, who was in his 20s when the elder philosopher was executed. The scion of an old Athenian family, Plato had been trying to decide whether to devote his life to politics or to writing tragic drama. After the death of Socrates, he rejected both possibilities. Instead, he invented a new kind of writing. Plato had a long and productive life, founding the Academy where people came from all over the world to study and leaving behind a large body of work. He did not write technical treatises of the sort later composed by his student Aristotle. Instead he dramatized conversations in concrete situations where characters discuss matters of common concern. In all his earliest work and much that came later, Socrates plays the central role. However, he raises more questions than he answers. Even where he develops a positive argument, Socrates often turns around to show its difficulties before the dialogue is done.

Scholars have argued for over two millennia whether Plato's dialogues are faithful to the historical Socrates or whether he adopted his teacher as the mouthpiece for his own views. (Socrates's contemporaries, the comic playwright Aristophanes and the historian Xenophon, left rather different portraits.) There is some consensus that Plato's earlier works are closest to representing Socrates. This volume offers a rich selection of these texts. Among them are three that depict events surrounding Socrates's trial. Because most Athenian readers would have their own memories of these events, Plato is unlikely to have strayed too far from historical truth. The *Apology* presents the speech that Socrates may have made in his own defense before about five hundred of his fellow citizens, the jurors at his trial. *Euthyphro* dramatizes an encounter outside the court between Socrates, who is about to be tried, and Euthyphro, who is about to accuse his own father of murder. *Crito* is set in the Athenian prison a few days before Socrates's execution. Regardless of their historical accuracy, these short dialogues raise central questions in ethics and political thought. With Euthyphro, Socrates investigates the meaning of *piety;* with Crito, whether it is just to break the laws of democratic Athens by escaping his unjust conviction. In his defense speech, he offers an account of his mission in life and its relation to his fellow citizens.

It all started at the Temple of Apollo In Delphi. One of his friends approached the oracle with the question: "Is anyone wiser than Socrates?" The answer was "No." Socrates was profoundly puzzled by this episode. He claimed to know nothing of any importance, so Socrates set off in search of someone wiser than himself. He interrogated the politicians, the poets, and the craftsmen. The first group turned out to know nothing of any account but believed themselves the wisest of men; the second could move men with powerful words but were unable to explain their meaning; the third group displayed expertise in their specialties but erred in claiming a more general wisdom. These conversations led Socrates to conclude that the oracle may have been correct in its riddling way: Socrates was wise in that he knew that he knew nothing, whereas others were unaware of their own ignorance.

In Plato's *Apology,* Socrates not only defends himself against the charges but also defines a new kind of wisdom. He cannot be guilty of "impiety," as he lived his life in service to Apollo; he is not guilty of "corrupting the youth," as he possesses no wisdom to teach. Socratic method is to question others about the ideas that guide their lives, whereas Socratic wisdom consists in knowing that you know nothing. Provoking others to think about what makes for a good life is the mission Apollo assigned to Socrates. Of course, we must also be aware of the possibility of Socratic irony—that he knows more than he says. His version of ignorance eclipses the knowledge of the wise men of Athens. Although he emphasizes his respect for the city, its gods, and its laws, Socrates appeals to something higher when he insists he would refuse any command to stop his questioning: "The unexamined life is not worth living."

In the *Apology*, Socrates offers his own explanation of how he got into trouble. Young people listening to his very public interrogation of their elders concluded that the leaders of their city were ignorant. Worse yet, they imitated Socrates's method by challenging their parents, teachers, and priests to justify and defend their claims to wisdom. Irritated and unhappy with such displays of intellectual independence, some concluded that Socrates's attitude implied a lack of respect that extended even to the gods. Socratic piety offered a profound challenge to the political and ethical beliefs of his city, where showing the young how to question authority amounted to corrupting them. On his own account, Socrates had no teaching with which to replace the "conventional wisdom." Plato knew full well the potential conflict between the philosopher and his city, between the active search for wisdom and passive deference to established opinion.

The other dialogues included here offer a more complex portrayal of Socrates and his method. The subjects that he investigated varied widely, but Socrates displayed little interest in the philosophy of nature that had already initiated scientific speculation among the Greeks. His concerns were closer to those of the Sophists, traveling wise men who arrived in Athens periodically to teach practical skills of active citizenship and oral advocacy for a fee. Although he examined similar questions, Socrates denied having the answers, taught no rhetorical skills, and did not accept payment. However, Socrates implicitly challenged the claims of these outsiders to teach civic virtue and practical wisdom. Socrates was an Athenian citizen engaging his fellows in critical conversation. In *Laches*, he discusses the meaning of courage with a couple of retired generals seeking instruction for their kinsmen. In *Lysis*, Socrates joins a

SOCRATIC METHOD?

group of young friends in trying to define *friendship*. In *Charmides*, he engages another such group in examining the widely celebrated virtue of *sophrosune*, the "temperance" that combines self-control and self-knowledge. (Plato's readers would know that the bright young man who gives his name to the latter dialogue would grow up to become one of the notorious Thirty Tyrants who briefly ruled Athens after its defeat by Sparta in the Peloponnesian War.) None of these dialogues reaches definite conclusions. They end in *aporia*, contradictions or other difficulties. The Socratic dialogues are aporetic: his interlocutors are left puzzled about what they thought they knew. Socrates's cross-examination, or *elenchus*, exposes their ignorance, but he exhorts his fellows to "care for their souls" by continuing to examine the ideals that guide their lives.

Socrates's practice of philosophy raised even deeper questions for Plato concerning the nature of knowledge, reality, and goodness itself. The commitment to shared inquiry assumes some link between logically investigating conceptions of human virtue and being able to make the right decisions and live a good life: "To know the good is to do the good."

Gorgias is the longest and most complex of the dialogues in this collection. In part, it is Plato's effort to show the differences between Socrates and the Sophist Gorgias; it also raises tough questions about the relations between seeking the truth and exercising power. Socrates challenges the Sophist to explain what he teaches and to defend the basis of his expertise. Socrates tries to show that rhetoric is not a form of knowledge but rather a knack for pleasing one's audience. Gorgias and his associates retort that being able to shape the opinions of one's fellow citizens is a source of power in the Athenian assembly and law courts. The ability to manipulate the opinions of others is a valuable weapon in the struggle to get what one wants in life. Socrates contests the ethical assumptions underlying this appeal to power and the pleasures it may bring. At one point, Gorgias's colleague Polus claims that a command of rhetoric allows one to triumph in court, even against just charges. Socrates suggests that an individual who has committed unjust acts should actually seek punishment to correct wrongs and restore justice to the psyche. Outraged by this suggestion, which flies in the face of Athenian conventional wisdom, Callicles highjacks the conversation to denounce Socratic philosophy as childish and dangerous.

The encounter between Socrates and Callicles exposes the tensions underlying the relation of the philosopher to his city and resonates with history. Callicles becomes the spokesperson for Athenian public opinion, which regards winning as an end in itself. When he virtually threatens Socrates with legal execution, the philosopher claims that any such trial would be like that of a doctor charged by a pastry chef in front of a jury of children. The conflict between philosophy and politics is played out here with the gloves off. Socrates goes beyond the earlier dialogues to articulate a positive conception of human excellence as guided by the love of goodness and truth rather than the appetite for power and pleasure. He begins to develop a model of justice as reflecting balance in the individual soul rather than the decisions of courts or legislatures. The just person achieves the happiness that comes from being able to live in harmony with one's self. (For reasons of space, we have omitted the myth of life after death with which the dialogue concludes.) Written later than the other texts here, *Gorgias* marks Plato's move away from aporetic Socratic dialogues towards the longer literary masterpieces of his middle period, such as *The Republic,* where Socrates constructs a city in speech to show his interlocutors the meaning of justice.

The dramatic confrontation in *Gorgias* demonstrates the violence that may be threatened or used to enforce the city's opinions

about how people should live. For Socrates, justice amounts to more than legality. Individuals who insist on thinking for themselves may come into conflict with the law. The stakes are high. As Plato shows in *Crito*, not all of Socrates's investigations were inconclusive. Socrates refused to abandon the conviction that it is better to suffer than to perpetrate an injustice. When his argument led to the conclusion that it would be wrong for a citizen to break the laws of democratic Athens, Socrates refused to flee. His commitment to the examined life led him to accept his own death rather than commit an act he believed to be wrong.
—*MBK*

Note. These translations are the work of Benjamin Jowett, whose two-volume *Collected Dialogues of Plato* (1871) remained the standard text until the 1960s. As Master of Balliol College, Oxford, Jowett installed classical "Greats" at the heart of elite education to instill ethical principles in future leaders of the British Empire. It is a tribute to the reach of Socratic method that his example also inspired Martin Luther King Jr.'s defense of civil disobedience in *Letter from a Birmingham Jail.*

The
SOCRATIC
DIALOGUES

EUTHYPHRO

PERSONS OF THE DIALOGUE: Socrates, Euthyphro.
SCENE: The Porch of the King Archon.

EUTHYPHRO: Why have you left the Lyceum, Socrates? and what are you doing in the Porch of the King Archon? Surely you cannot be concerned in a suit before the King, like myself?

SOCRATES: Not in a suit, Euthyphro; impeachment is the word which the Athenians use.

EUTHYPHRO: What! I suppose that someone has been prosecuting you, for I cannot believe that you are the prosecutor of another.

SOCRATES: Certainly not.

EUTHYPHRO: Then someone else has been prosecuting you?

SOCRATES: Yes.

EUTHYPHRO: And who is he?

SOCRATES: A young man who is little known, Euthyphro; and I hardly know him: his name is Meletus, and he is of the deme of Pitthis. Perhaps you may remember his appearance; he has a beak, and long straight hair, and a beard which is ill grown.

EUTHYPHRO: No, I do not remember him, Socrates. But what is the charge which he brings against you?

SOCRATES: What is the charge? Well, a very serious charge, which shows a good deal of character in the young man, and for which he is certainly not to be despised. He says he knows how the youth are corrupted and who are their corruptors. I fancy that he must be a wise man, and seeing that I am the reverse of a wise man, he has found me out, and is going to accuse me of corrupting his young friends. And of this our mother the state is to be the judge. Of all our political men he is the only one who seems to me to begin in the right way, with the cultivation of virtue in youth; like a good husbandman, he makes the young shoots his first care, and clears away us who are the destroyers of them. This is only the first step; he will afterwards attend to the elder branches; and if he goes on as he has begun, he will be a very great public benefactor.

EUTHYPHRO: I hope that he may; but I rather fear, Socrates, that the opposite will turn out to be the truth. My opinion is that in attacking you he is simply aiming a blow at the foundation of the state. But in what way does he say that you corrupt the young?

SOCRATES: He brings a wonderful accusation against me, which at first hearing excites surprise: he says that I am a poet or maker of gods, and that I invent new gods and deny the existence of old ones; this is the ground of his indictment.

EUTHYPHRO: I understand, Socrates; he means to attack you about the familiar sign which occasionally, as you say, comes to you. He thinks that you are a neologian, and he is going to have you up before the court for this. He knows that such a charge is readily received by the world, as I myself know too well; for when I speak in the assembly about divine things, and foretell the future to them, they laugh at me and think me a madman. Yet every word that I say is true. But they are jealous of us all; and we must be brave and go at them.

SOCRATES: Their laughter, friend Euthyphro, is not a matter of much consequence. For a man may be thought wise; but the Athenians, I suspect, do not much trouble themselves about him until he begins to impart his wisdom to others, and then for some reason or other, perhaps, as you say, from jealousy, they are angry.

EUTHYPHRO: I am never likely to try their temper in this way.

SOCRATES: I dare say not, for you are reserved in your behaviour, and seldom impart your wisdom. But I have a benevolent habit of pouring out myself to everybody, and would even pay for a listener, and I am afraid that the Athenians may think me too talkative. Now if, as I was saying, they would only laugh at me, as you say that they laugh at you, the time might pass gaily enough in the court; but perhaps they may be in earnest, and then what the end will be you soothsayers only can predict.

EUTHYPHRO: I dare say that the affair will end in nothing, Socrates, and that you will win your cause; and I think that I shall win my own.

SOCRATES: And what is your suit, Euthyphro? Are you the pursuer or the defendant?

EUTHYPHRO: I am the pursuer.

SOCRATES: Of whom?

EUTHYPHRO: You will think me mad when I tell you.

SOCRATES: Why, has the fugitive wings?

EUTHYPHRO: Nay, he is not very volatile at his time of life.

SOCRATES: Who is he?

EUTHYPHRO: My father.

SOCRATES: Your father! My good man?

EUTHYPHRO: Yes.

SOCRATES: And of what is he accused?

EUTHYPHRO: Of murder, Socrates.

SOCRATES: By the powers, Euthyphro! How little does the common herd know of the nature of right and truth. A man must be an extraordinary man, and have made great strides in wisdom, before he could have seen his way to bring such an action.

EUTHYPHRO: Indeed, Socrates, he must.

SOCRATES: I suppose that the man whom your father murdered was one of your relatives—clearly he was; for if he had been a stranger you would never have thought of prosecuting him.

EUTHYPHRO: I am amused, Socrates, at your making a distinction between one who is a relation and one who is not a relation; for surely the pollution is the same in either case, if you knowingly associate with the murderer when you ought to clear yourself and him by proceeding against him. The real question is whether the murdered man has been justly slain. If justly, then your duty is to let the matter alone; but if unjustly, then even if the murderer lives under the same roof with you and eats at the same table, proceed against him. Now the man who is dead was a poor dependant of mine who worked for us as a field labourer on our farm in Naxos, and one day in a fit of drunken passion he got into a quarrel with one of our domestic servants and slew him. My father bound him hand and foot and threw him into a ditch, and then sent to Athens to ask of a diviner what he should do with him. Meanwhile he never attended to him and took no care about him, for he regarded him as a murderer; and thought that no great harm would be done even if he did die. Now this was just what happened. For such was the effect of cold and hunger and chains upon him, that before the messenger returned from the diviner, he was dead. And my father and family are angry with me for taking the part of the murderer and prosecuting my father. They say that he did not kill him, and that if he did, the dead man was but a murderer, and I ought not to take any notice, for that a son is impious who prosecutes a father. Which shows, Socrates, how little they know what the gods think about piety and impiety.

SOCRATES: Good heavens, Euthyphro! and is your knowledge of religion and of things pious and impious so very exact, that, supposing the circumstances to be as you state them, you are not afraid lest you too may be doing an impious thing in bringing an action against your father?

EUTHYPHRO: The best of Euthyphro, and that which distinguishes him, Socrates, from other men, is his exact knowledge of all such matters. What should I be good for without it?

SOCRATES: Rare friend! I think that I cannot do better than be your disciple. Then before the trial with Meletus comes on I shall challenge him, and say that I have always had a great interest in religious questions, and now, as he charges me with rash imaginations and innovations in religion, I have become your disciple. You, Meletus, as I shall say to him, acknowledge Euthyphro to be a great theologian, and sound in his opinions; and if you approve of him you ought to approve of me, and not have me into court; but if you disapprove, you should begin by indicting him who is my teacher, and who will be the ruin, not of the young, but of the old; that is to say, of myself whom he instructs, and of his old father whom he admonishes and chastises. And if Meletus refuses to listen to me, but will go on, and will not shift the indictment from me to you, I cannot do better than repeat this challenge in the court.

EUTHYPHRO

EUTHYPHRO: Yes, indeed, Socrates; and if he attempts to indict me I am mistaken if I do not find a flaw in him; the court shall have a great deal more to say to him than to me.

SOCRATES: And I, my dear friend, knowing this, am desirous of becoming your disciple. For I observe that no one appears to notice you—not even this Meletus; but his sharp eyes have found me out at once, and he has indicted me for impiety. And therefore, I adjure you to tell me the nature of piety and impiety, which you said that you knew so well, and of murder, and of other offences against the gods. What are they? Is not piety in every action always the same? and impiety, again—is it not always the opposite of piety, and also the same with itself, having, as impiety, one notion which includes whatever is impious?

EUTHYPHRO: To be sure, Socrates.

SOCRATES: And what is piety, and what is impiety?

EUTHYPHRO: Piety is doing as I am doing; that is to say, prosecuting any one who is guilty of murder, sacrilege, or of any similar crime—whether he be your father or mother, or whoever he may be—that makes no difference; and not to prosecute them is impiety. And please to consider, Socrates, what a notable proof I will give you of the truth of my words, a proof which I have already given to others: of the principle, I mean, that the impious, whoever he may be, ought not to go unpunished. For do not men regard Zeus as the best and most righteous of the gods?—and yet they admit that he bound his father (Cronos) because he wickedly devoured his sons, and that he too had punished his own father (Uranus) for a similar reason, in a nameless manner. And yet when I proceed against my father, they are angry with me. So inconsistent are they in their way of talking when the gods are concerned, and when I am concerned.

SOCRATES: May not this be the reason, Euthyphro, why I am charged with impiety—that I cannot away with these stories about the gods? And therefore I suppose that people think me wrong. But, as you who are well informed about them approve of them, I cannot do better than assent to your superior wisdom. What else can I say, confessing as I do, that I know nothing about them? Tell me, for the love of Zeus, whether you really believe that they are true.

EUTHYPHRO: Yes, Socrates; and things more wonderful still, of which the world is in ignorance.

SOCRATES: And do you really believe that the gods fought with one another, and had dire quarrels, battles, and the like, as the poets say, and as you may see represented in the works of great artists? The temples are full of them; and notably the robe of Athene, which is carried up to the Acropolis at the great Panathenaea, is embroidered with them. Are all these tales of the gods true, Euthyphro?

EUTHYPHRO: Yes, Socrates; and, as I was saying, I can tell you, if you would like to hear them, many other things about the gods which would quite amaze you.

SOCRATES: I dare say; and you shall tell me them at some other time when I have leisure. But just at present I would rather hear from you a more precise answer, which you have not as yet given, my friend, to the question, What is 'piety'? When asked, you only replied, 'Doing as you do, charging your father with murder.'

EUTHYPHRO: And what I said was true, Socrates.

SOCRATES: No doubt, Euthyphro; but you would admit that there are many other pious acts?

EUTHYPHRO: There are.

SOCRATES: Remember that I did not ask you to give me two or three examples of piety, but to explain the general idea which makes all pious things to be pious. Do you not recollect that there was one idea which made the impious impious, and the pious pious?

EUTHYPHRO: I remember.

SOCRATES: Tell me what is the nature of this idea, and then I shall have a standard to which I may look, and by which I may measure actions, whether yours or those of any one else, and then I shall be able to say that such and such an action is pious, such another impious.

EUTHYPHRO: I will tell you, if you like.

SOCRATES: I should very much like.

EUTHYPHRO: Piety, then, is that which is dear to the gods, and impiety is that which is not dear to them.

SOCRATES: Very good, Euthyphro; you have now given me the sort of answer which I wanted. But whether what you say is true or not I cannot as yet tell, although I make no doubt that you will prove the truth of your words.

EUTHYPHRO: Of course.

SOCRATES: Come, then, and let us examine what we are saying. That thing or person which is dear to the gods is pious, and that thing or person which is hateful to the gods is impious, these two being the extreme opposites of one another. Was not that said?

EUTHYPHRO: It was.

SOCRATES: And well said?

EUTHYPHRO: Yes, Socrates, I thought so; it was certainly said.

SOCRATES: And further, Euthyphro, the gods were admitted to have enmities and hatreds and differences?

EUTHYPHRO: Yes, that was also said.

SOCRATES: And what sort of difference creates enmity and anger? Suppose for example that you and I, my good friend, differ about a number; do differences of this sort make us enemies and set us at variance with one another? Do we not go at once to arithmetic, and put an end to them by a sum?

EUTHYPHRO: True.

SOCRATES: Or suppose that we differ about magnitudes, do we not quickly end the differences by measuring?

EUTHYPHRO: Very true.

SOCRATES: And we end a controversy about heavy and light by resorting to a weighing machine?

EUTHYPHRO: To be sure.

SOCRATES: But what differences are there which cannot be thus decided, and which therefore make us angry and set us at enmity with one another? I dare say the answer does not occur to you at the moment, and therefore I will suggest that these enmities arise when the matters of difference are the just and unjust, good and evil, honourable and dishonourable. Are not these the points about which men differ, and about which when we are unable satisfactorily to decide our differences, you and I and all of us quarrel, when we do quarrel?

EUTHYPHRO: Yes, Socrates, the nature of the differences about which we quarrel is such as you describe.

SOCRATES: And the quarrels of the gods, noble Euthyphro, when they occur, are of a like nature?

EUTHYPHRO: Certainly they are.

SOCRATES: They have differences of opinion, as you say, about good and evil, just and unjust, honourable and dishonourable: there would have been no quarrels among them, if there had been no such differences—would there now?

EUTHYPHRO: You are quite right.

SOCRATES: Does not every man love that which he deems noble and just and good, and hate the opposite of them?

EUTHYPHRO: Very true.

SOCRATES: But, as you say, people regard the same things, some as just and others as unjust—about these they dispute; and so there arise wars and fightings among them.

EUTHYPHRO: Very true.

SOCRATES: Then the same things are hated by the gods and loved by the gods, and are both hateful and dear to them?

EUTHYPHRO: True.

SOCRATES: And upon this view the same things, Euthyphro, will be pious and also impious?

EUTHYPHRO: So I should suppose.

SOCRATES: Then, my friend, I remark with surprise that you have not answered the question which I asked. For I certainly did not ask you to tell me what action is both pious and impious: but now it would seem that what is loved by the gods is also hated by them. And therefore, Euthyphro, in thus chastising your father you may very likely be doing what is agreeable to Zeus but disagreeable to Cronos or Uranus, and what is acceptable to Hephaestus but unacceptable to Hera, and there may be other gods who have similar differences of opinion.

EUTHYPHRO: But I believe, Socrates, that all the gods would be agreed as to the propriety of punishing a murderer: there would be no difference of opinion about that.

SOCRATES: Well, but speaking of men, Euthyphro, did you ever hear anyone arguing that a murderer or any sort of evil-doer ought to be let off?

EUTHYPHRO: I should rather say that these are the questions which they are always arguing, especially in courts of law: they commit all sorts of crimes, and there is nothing which they will not do or say in their own defense.

SOCRATES: But do they admit their guilt, Euthyphro, and yet say that they ought not to be punished?

EUTHYPHRO: No; they do not.

SOCRATES: Then there are some things which they do not venture to say and do: for they do not venture to argue that the guilty are to be unpunished, but they deny their guilt, do they not?

EUTHYPHRO: Yes.

SOCRATES: Then they do not argue that the evil-doer should not be punished, but they argue about the fact of who the evil-doer is, and what he did and when?

EUTHYPHRO: True.

SOCRATES: And the gods are in the same case, if as you assert they quarrel about just and unjust, and some of them say while others deny that injustice is done among them.

For surely neither God nor man will ever venture to say that the doer of injustice is not to be punished?

EUTHYPHRO: That is true, Socrates, in the main.

SOCRATES: But they join issue about the particulars—gods and men alike; and, if they dispute at all, they dispute about some act which is called in question, and which by some is affirmed to be just, by others to be unjust. Is not that true?

EUTHYPHRO: Quite true.

SOCRATES: Well then, my dear friend Euthyphro, do tell me, for my better instruction and information, what proof have you that in the opinion of all the gods a servant who is guilty of murder, and is put in chains by the master of the dead man, and dies because he is put in chains before he who bound him can learn from the interpreters of the gods what he ought to do with him, dies unjustly; and that on behalf of such a one a son ought to proceed against his father and accuse him of murder. How would you show that all the gods absolutely agree in approving of his act? Prove to me that they do, and I will applaud your wisdom as long as I live.

EUTHYPHRO: It will be a difficult task; but I could make the matter very clear indeed to you.

SOCRATES: I understand; you mean to say that I am not so quick of apprehension as the judges: for to them you will be sure to prove that the act is unjust, and hateful to the gods.

EUTHYPHRO: Yes indeed, Socrates; at least if they will listen to me.

SOCRATES: But they will be sure to listen if they find that you are a good speaker. There was a notion that came into my mind while you were speaking; I said to myself: 'Well, and what if Euthyphro does prove to me that all the gods regarded the death of the serf as unjust, how do I know anything more of the nature of piety and impiety? For granting that this action may be hateful to the gods, still piety and impiety are not adequately defined by these distinctions, for that which is hateful to the gods has been shown to be also pleasing and dear to them.' And therefore, Euthyphro, I do not ask you to prove this; I will suppose, if you like, that all the gods condemn and abominate such an action. But I will amend the definition so far as to say that what all the gods hate is impious, and what they love pious or holy; and what some of them love and others hate is both or neither. Shall this be our definition of piety and impiety?

EUTHYPHRO: Why not, Socrates?

SOCRATES: Why not! Certainly, as far as I am concerned, Euthyphro, there is no reason why not. But whether this admission will greatly assist you in the task of instructing me as you promised, is a matter for you to consider.

EUTHYPHRO: Yes, I should say that what all the gods love is pious and holy, and the opposite which they all hate, impious.

SOCRATES: Ought we to inquire into the truth of this, Euthyphro, or simply to accept the mere statement on our own authority and that of others? What do you say?

EUTHYPHRO: We should inquire; and I believe that the statement will stand the test of inquiry.

SOCRATES: We shall know better, my good friend, in a little while. The point which I should first wish to understand is whether the pious or holy is beloved by the gods because it is holy, or holy because it is beloved of the gods.

EUTHYPHRO: I do not understand your meaning, Socrates.

SOCRATES: I will endeavour to explain: we speak of carrying and we speak of being carried, of leading and being led, seeing and being seen. You know that in all such cases there is a difference, and you know also in what the difference lies?

EUTHYPHRO: I think that I understand.

SOCRATES: And is not that which is beloved distinct from that which loves?

EUTHYPHRO: Certainly.

SOCRATES: Well; and now tell me, is that which is carried in this state of carrying because it is carried, or for some other reason?

EUTHYPHRO: No; that is the reason.

SOCRATES: And the same is true of what is led and of what is seen?

EUTHYPHRO: True.

SOCRATES: And a thing is not seen because it is visible, but conversely, visible because it is seen; nor is a thing led because it is in the state of being led, or carried because it is in the state of being carried, but the converse of this. And now I think, Euthyphro, that my meaning will be intelligible; and my meaning is, that any state of action or passion implies previous action or passion. It does not become because it is becoming, but it is in a state of becoming because it becomes; neither does it suffer because it is in a state of suffering, but it is in a state of suffering because it suffers. Do you not agree?

EUTHYPHRO: Yes.

SOCRATES: Is not that which is loved in some state either of becoming or suffering?

EUTHYPHRO: Yes.

SOCRATES: And the same holds as in the previous instances; the state of being loved follows the act of being loved, and not the act the state.

EUTHYPHRO: Certainly.

SOCRATES: And what do you say of piety, Euthyphro: is not piety, according to your definition, loved by all the gods?

EUTHYPHRO: Yes.

SOCRATES: Because it is pious or holy, or for some other reason?

EUTHYPHRO: No, that is the reason.

SOCRATES: It is loved because it is holy, not holy because it is loved?

EUTHYPHRO: Yes.

SOCRATES: And that which is dear to the gods is loved by them, and is in a state to be loved of them because it is loved of them?

EUTHYPHRO: Certainly.

SOCRATES: Then that which is dear to the gods, Euthyphro, is not holy, nor is that which is holy loved of God, as you affirm; but they are two different things.

EUTHYPHRO: How do you mean, Socrates?

SOCRATES: I mean to say that the holy has been acknowledged by us to be loved of God because it is holy, not to be holy because it is loved.

EUTHYPHRO: Yes.

SOCRATES: But that which is dear to the gods is dear to them because it is loved by them, not loved by them because it is dear to them.

EUTHYPHRO: True.

SOCRATES: But, friend Euthyphro, if that which is holy is the same with that which is dear to God, and is loved because it is holy, then that which is dear to God would have been loved as being dear to God; but if that which is dear to God is dear to him because loved by him, then that which is holy would have been holy because loved by him. But now you see that the reverse is the case, and that they are quite different from one another. For one (theophiles) is of a kind to be loved cause it is loved, and the other (osion) is loved because it is of a kind to be loved. Thus you appear to me, Euthyphro, when I ask you what is the essence of holiness, to offer an attribute only, and not the essence—the attribute of being loved by all the gods. But you still refuse to explain to me the nature of holiness. And therefore, if you please, I will ask you not to hide your treasure, but to tell me once more what holiness or piety really is, whether dear to the gods or not (for that is a matter about which we will not quarrel); and what is impiety?

EUTHYPHRO: I really do not know, Socrates, how to express what I mean. For somehow or other our arguments, on whatever ground we rest them, seem to turn round and walk away from us.

SOCRATES: Your words, Euthyphro, are like the handiwork of my ancestor Daedalus; and if I were the sayer or propounder of them, you might say that my arguments walk away and will not remain fixed where they are placed because I am a descendant of his. But now, since these notions are your own, you must find some other gibe, for they certainly, as you yourself allow, show an inclination to be on the move.

EUTHYPHRO: Nay, Socrates, I shall still say that you are the Daedalus who sets arguments in motion; not I, certainly, but you make them move or go round, for they would never have stirred, as far as I am concerned.

SOCRATES: Then I must be a greater than Daedalus: for whereas he only made his own inventions to move, I move those of other people as well. And the beauty of it is, that I would rather not. For I would give the wisdom of Daedalus, and the wealth of Tantalus, to be able to detain them and keep them fixed. But enough of this. As I perceive that you are lazy, I will myself endeavour to show you how you might instruct me in the nature of piety; and I hope that you will not grudge your labour. Tell me, then—Is not that which is pious necessarily just?

EUTHYPHRO: Yes.

SOCRATES: And is, then, all which is just pious? or, is that which is pious all just, but that which is just, only in part and not all, pious?

EUTHYPHRO: I do not understand you, Socrates.

SOCRATES: And yet I know that you are as much wiser than I am, as you are younger. But, as I was saying, revered friend, the abundance of your wisdom makes you lazy. Please to exert yourself, for there is no real difficulty in understanding me. What I mean I may explain by an illustration of what I do not mean. The poet (Stasinus) sings—

'Of Zeus, the author and creator of all these things, You will not tell: for where there is fear there is also reverence.' Now I disagree with this poet. Shall I tell you in what respect?

EUTHYPHRO: By all means.

SOCRATES: I should not say that where there is fear there is also reverence; for I am sure that many persons fear poverty and disease, and the like evils, but I do not perceive that they reverence the objects of their fear.

EUTHYPHRO: Very true.

SOCRATES: But where reverence is, there is fear; for he who has a feeling of reverence and shame about the commission of any action, fears and is afraid of an ill reputation.

EUTHYPHRO: No doubt.

SOCRATES: Then we are wrong in saying that where there is fear there is also reverence; and we should say, where there is reverence there is also fear. But there is not always reverence where there is fear; for fear is a more extended notion, and reverence is a part of fear, just as the odd is a part of number, and number is a more extended notion than the odd. I suppose that you follow me now?

EUTHYPHRO: Quite well.

SOCRATES: That was the sort of question which I meant to raise when I asked whether the just is always the pious, or the pious always the just; and whether there may not be justice where there is not piety; for justice is the more extended notion of which piety is only a part. Do you dissent?

EUTHYPHRO: No, I think that you are quite right.

SOCRATES: Then, if piety is a part of justice, I suppose that we should inquire what part? If you had pursued the inquiry in the previous cases; for instance, if you had asked me what is an even number, and what part of number the even is, I should have had no difficulty in replying, a number which represents a figure having two equal sides. Do you not agree?

EUTHYPHRO: Yes, I quite agree.

SOCRATES: In like manner, I want you to tell me what part of justice is piety or holiness, that I may be able to tell Meletus not to do me injustice, or indict me for impiety, as I am now adequately instructed by you in the nature of piety or holiness, and their opposites.

EUTHYPHRO: Piety or holiness, Socrates, appears to me to be that part of justice which attends to the gods, as there is the other part of justice which attends to men.

SOCRATES: That is good, Euthyphro; yet still there is a little point about which I should like to have further information. What is the meaning of 'attention'? For attention can hardly be used in the same sense when applied to the gods as when applied to other things. For instance, horses are said to require attention, and not every person is able to attend to them, but only a person skilled in horsemanship. Is it not so?

EUTHYPHRO: Certainly.

SOCRATES: I should suppose that the art of horsemanship is the art of attending to horses?

EUTHYPHRO: Yes.

SOCRATES: Nor is every one qualified to attend to dogs, but only the huntsman?

EUTHYPHRO: True.

SOCRATES: And I should also conceive that the art of the huntsman is the art of attending to dogs?

EUTHYPHRO: Yes.

SOCRATES: As the art of the oxherd is the art of attending to oxen?

EUTHYPHRO: Very true.

SOCRATES: In like manner holiness or piety is the art of attending to the gods?—that would be your meaning, Euthyphro?

EUTHYPHRO: Yes.

SOCRATES: And is not attention always designed for the good or benefit of that to which the attention is given? As in the case of horses, you may observe that when attended to by the horseman's art they are benefited and improved, are they not?

EUTHYPHRO: True.

SOCRATES: As the dogs are benefited by the huntsman's art, and the oxen by the art of the oxherd, and all other things are tended or attended for their good and not for their hurt?

EUTHYPHRO: Certainly, not for their hurt.

SOCRATES: But for their good?

EUTHYPHRO: Of course.

SOCRATES: And does piety or holiness, which has been defined to be the art of attending to the gods, benefit or improve them? Would you say that when you do a holy act you make any of the gods better?

EUTHYPHRO: No, no; that was certainly not what I meant.

SOCRATES: And I, Euthyphro, never supposed that you did. I asked you the question about the nature of the attention, because I thought that you did not.

EUTHYPHRO: You do me justice, Socrates; that is not the sort of attention which I mean.

SOCRATES: Good: but I must still ask what is this attention to the gods which is called piety?

EUTHYPHRO: It is such, Socrates, as servants show to their masters.

SOCRATES: I understand—a sort of ministration to the gods.

EUTHYPHRO: Exactly.

SOCRATES: Medicine is also a sort of ministration or service, having in view the attainment of some object—would you not say of health?

EUTHYPHRO: I should.

SOCRATES: Again, there is an art which ministers to the ship-builder with a view to the attainment of some result?

EUTHYPHRO: Yes, Socrates, with a view to the building of a ship.

SOCRATES: As there is an art which ministers to the house-builder with a view to the building of a house?

EUTHYPHRO: Yes.

SOCRATES: And now tell me, my good friend, about the art which ministers to the gods: what work does that help to accomplish? For you must surely know if, as you say, you are of all men living the one who is best instructed in religion.

EUTHYPHRO: And I speak the truth, Socrates.

SOCRATES: Tell me then, oh tell me—what is that fair work which the gods do by the help of our ministrations?

EUTHYPHRO: Many and fair, Socrates, are the works which they do.

SOCRATES: Why, my friend, and so are those of a general. But the chief of them is easily told. Would you not say that victory in war is the chief of them?

EUTHYPHRO: Certainly.

SOCRATES: Many and fair, too, are the works of the husbandman, if I am not mistaken; but his chief work is the production of food from the earth?

EUTHYPHRO: Exactly.

SOCRATES: And of the many and fair things done by the gods, which is the chief or principal one?

EUTHYPHRO: I have told you already, Socrates, that to learn all these things accurately will be very tiresome. Let me simply say that piety or holiness is learning how to please the gods in word and deed, by prayers and sacrifices. Such piety is the salvation of families and states, just as the impious, which is unpleasing to the gods, is their ruin and destruction.

SOCRATES: I think that you could have answered in much fewer words the chief question which I asked, Euthyphro, if you had chosen. But I see plainly that you are not disposed to instruct me—clearly not: else why, when we reached the point, did you turn aside? Had you only answered me I should have truly learned of you by this time the nature of piety. Now, as the asker of a question is necessarily dependent on the answerer, whither he leads I must follow; and can only ask again, what is the pious, and what is piety? Do you mean that they are a sort of science of praying and sacrificing?

EUTHYPHRO: Yes, I do.

SOCRATES: And sacrificing is giving to the gods, and prayer is asking of the gods?

EUTHYPHRO: Yes, Socrates.

SOCRATES: Upon this view, then, piety is a science of asking and giving?

EUTHYPHRO: You understand me capitally, Socrates.

SOCRATES: Yes, my friend; the reason is that I am a votary of your science, and give my mind to it, and therefore nothing which you say will be thrown away upon me. Please then to tell me, what is the nature of this service to the gods? Do you mean that we prefer requests and give gifts to them?

EUTHYPHRO: Yes, I do.

SOCRATES: Is not the right way of asking to ask of them what we want?

EUTHYPHRO: Certainly.

SOCRATES: And the right way of giving is to give to them in return what they want of us. There would be no meaning in an art which gives to any one that which he does not want.

EUTHYPHRO: Very true, Socrates.

SOCRATES: Then piety, Euthyphro, is an art which gods and men have of doing business with one another?

EUTHYPHRO: That is an expression which you may use, if you like.

SOCRATES: But I have no particular liking for anything but the truth. I wish, however, that you would tell me what benefit accrues to the gods from our gifts. There is no doubt about what they give to us; for there is no good thing which they do not give; but how we can give any good thing to them in return is far from being equally clear. If they give everything and we give nothing, that must be an affair of business in which we have very greatly the advantage of them.

EUTHYPHRO: And do you imagine, Socrates, that any benefit accrues to the gods from our gifts?

SOCRATES: But if not, Euthyphro, what is the meaning of gifts which are conferred by us upon the gods?

EUTHYPHRO: What else, but tributes of honour; and, as I was just now saying, what pleases them?

SOCRATES: Piety, then, is pleasing to the gods, but not beneficial or dear to them?

EUTHYPHRO: I should say that nothing could be dearer.

SOCRATES: Then once more the assertion is repeated that piety is dear to the gods?

EUTHYPHRO: Certainly.

SOCRATES: And when you say this, can you wonder at your words not standing firm, but walking away? Will you accuse me of being the Daedalus who makes them walk away, not perceiving that there is another and far greater artist than Daedalus who makes them go round in a circle, and he is yourself; for the argument, as you will perceive, comes round to the same point. Were we not saying that the holy or pious was not the same with that which is loved of the gods? Have you forgotten?

EUTHYPHRO: I quite remember.

SOCRATES: And are you not saying that what is loved of the gods is holy; and is not this the same as what is dear to them—do you see?

EUTHYPHRO: True.

SOCRATES: Then either we were wrong in our former assertion; or, if we were right then, we are wrong now.

EUTHYPHRO: One of the two must be true.

SOCRATES: Then we must begin again and ask, 'What is piety?' That is an inquiry which I shall never be weary of pursuing as far as in me lies; and I entreat you not to scorn me, but to apply your mind to the utmost, and tell me the truth. For, if any man knows, you are he; and therefore I must detain you, like Proteus, until you tell. If you had not certainly known the nature of piety and impiety, I am confident that you would never, on behalf of a serf, have charged your aged father with murder. You would not have run such a risk of doing wrong in the sight of the gods, and you would have had too much respect for the opinions of men. I am sure, therefore, that you know the nature of piety and impiety. Speak out then, my dear Euthyphro, and do not hide your knowledge.

EUTHYPHRO: Another time, Socrates; for I am in a hurry, and must go now.

SOCRATES: Alas! my companion, and will you leave me in despair? I was hoping that you would instruct me in the nature of piety and impiety; and then I might have cleared myself of Meletus and his indictment. I would have told him that I had been enlightened by Euthyphro, and had given up rash innovations and speculations, in which I indulged only through ignorance, and that now I am about to lead a better life.

APOLOGY

How you, O Athenians, have been affected by my accusers, I cannot tell; but I know that they almost made me forget who I was—so persuasively did they speak; and yet they have hardly uttered a word of truth. But of the many falsehoods told by them, there was one which quite amazed me;—I mean when they said that you should be upon your guard and not allow yourselves to be deceived by the force of my eloquence. To say this, when they were certain to be detected as soon as I opened my lips and proved myself to be anything but a great speaker, did indeed appear to me most shameless—unless by the force of eloquence they mean the force of truth; for is such is their meaning, I admit that I am eloquent. But in how different a way from theirs! Well, as I was saying, they have scarcely spoken the truth at all; but from me you shall hear the whole truth: not, however, delivered after their manner in a set oration duly ornamented with words and phrases. No, by heaven! But I shall use the words and arguments which occur to me at the moment; for I am confident in the justice of my cause (Or, I am certain that I am right in taking this course.): at my time of life I ought not to be appearing before you, O men of Athens, in the character of a juvenile orator—let no one expect it of me. And I must beg of you to grant me a favour:—If I defend myself in my accustomed manner, and you hear me using the words which I have been in the habit of using in the agora, at the tables of the money-changers, or anywhere else, I would ask you not to be surprised, and not to interrupt me on this account. For I am more than seventy years of age, and appearing now for the first time in a court of law, I am quite a stranger to the language of the place; and therefore I would have you regard me as if I were really a stranger, whom you would excuse if he spoke in his native tongue, and after the fashion of his country:—Am I making an unfair request of you? Never mind the manner, which may or may not be good; but think only of the truth of my words, and give heed to that: let the speaker speak truly and the judge decide justly.

And first, I have to reply to the older charges and to my first accusers, and then I will go on to the later ones. For of old I have had many accusers, who have accused me falsely to you during many years; and I am more afraid of them than of Anytus and his associates, who are dangerous, too, in their own way. But far more dangerous are the others, who began when you were children, and took possession of your minds with their falsehoods, telling of one Socrates, a wise man, who speculated about the heaven above, and searched into the earth beneath, and made the worse appear the better cause. The disseminators of this tale are the accusers whom I dread; for their hearers are apt to fancy that such inquirers do not believe in the existence of the gods. And they are many, and their charges against me are of ancient date, and they were made by them in the days when you were more impressible than you are now—in childhood, or it may have been in youth—and the cause when heard went by default, for there was none to answer. And hardest of all, I do not know and cannot tell the names of my accusers; unless in the chance case of a Comic poet. All who from envy and malice have persuaded you—some of them having first convinced themselves—all this class of men are most difficult to deal with; for I cannot have them up here, and cross-examine them, and therefore I must simply fight with shadows in my own defense, and argue when there is no one who answers. I will ask you then to assume with me, as I was

APOLOGY

saying, that my opponents are of two kinds; one recent, the other ancient: and I hope that you will see the propriety of my answering the latter first, for these accusations you heard long before the others, and much oftener.

Well, then, I must make my defense, and endeavour to clear away in a short time, a slander which has lasted a long time. May I succeed, if to succeed be for my good and yours, or likely to avail me in my cause! The task is not an easy one; I quite understand the nature of it. And so leaving the event with God, in obedience to the law I will now make my defense.

I will begin at the beginning, and ask what is the accusation which has given rise to the slander of me, and in fact has encouraged Meletus to proof this charge against me. Well, what do the slanderers say? They shall be my prosecutors, and I will sum up their words in an affidavit: 'Socrates is an evil-doer, and a curious person, who searches into things under the earth and in heaven, and he makes the worse appear the better cause; and he teaches the aforesaid doctrines to others.' Such is the nature of the accusation: it is just what you have yourselves seen in the comedy of Aristophanes,[†] who has introduced a man whom he calls Socrates, going about and saying that he walks in air, and talking a deal of nonsense concerning matters of which I do not pretend to know either much or little—not that I mean to speak disparagingly of any one who is a student of natural philosophy. I should be very sorry if Meletus could bring so grave a charge against me. But the simple truth is, O Athenians, that I have nothing to do with physical speculations. Very many of those here present are witnesses to the truth of this, and to them I appeal. Speak then, you who have heard me, and tell

[†]Aristoph., Clouds.

your neighbours whether any of you have ever known me hold forth in few words or in many upon such matters...You hear their answer. And from what they say of this part of the charge you will be able to judge of the truth of the rest. As little foundation is there for the report that I am a teacher, and take money; this accusation has no more truth in it than the other. Although, if a man were really able to instruct mankind, to receive money for giving instruction would, in my opinion, be an honour to him. There is Gorgias of Leontium, and Prodicus of Ceos, and Hippias of Elis, who go the round of the cities, and are able to persuade the young men to leave their own citizens by whom they might be taught for nothing, and come to them whom they not only pay, but are thankful if they may be allowed to pay them. There is at this time a Parian philosopher residing in Athens, of whom I have heard; and I came to hear of him in this way: I came across a man who has spent a world of money on the Sophists, Callias, the son of Hipponicus, and knowing that he had sons, I asked him: 'Callias,' I said, 'if your two sons were foals or calves, there would be no difficulty in finding someone to put over them; we should hire a trainer of horses, or a farmer probably, who would improve and perfect them in their own proper virtue and excellence; but as they are human beings, whom are you thinking of placing over them? Is there any one who understands human and political virtue? You must have thought about the matter, for you have sons; is there any one?' 'There is,' he said. 'Who is he?' said I; 'and of what country? and what does he charge?' 'Evenus the Parian,' he replied; 'he is the man, and his charge is five minae.' Happy is Evenus, I said to myself, if he really has this wisdom, and teaches at such a moderate charge. Had I the same, I should have been very proud and conceited; but the truth is that I have no knowledge of the kind.

I dare say, Athenians, that someone among you will reply, 'Yes, Socrates, but what is the origin of these accusations which are brought against you; there must have been something strange which you have been doing? All these rumours and this talk about you would never have arisen if you had been like other men: tell us, then, what is the cause of them, for we should be sorry to judge hastily of you.' Now I regard this as a fair challenge, and I will endeavour to explain to you the reason why I am called wise and have such an evil fame. Please to attend then. And although some of you may think that I am joking, I declare that I will tell you the entire truth. Men of Athens, this reputation of mine has come of a certain sort of wisdom which I possess. If you ask me what kind of wisdom, I reply, wisdom such as may perhaps be attained by man, for to that extent I am inclined to believe that I am wise; whereas the persons of whom I was speaking have a superhuman wisdom which I may fail to describe, because I have it not myself; and he who says that I have, speaks falsely, and is taking away my character. And here, O men of Athens, I must beg you not to interrupt me, even if I seem to say something extravagant. For the word which I will speak is not mine. I will refer you to a witness who is worthy of credit; that witness shall be the God of Delphi—he will tell you about my wisdom, if I have any, and of what sort it is. You must have known Chaerephon; he was early a friend of mine, and also a friend of yours, for he shared in the recent exile of the people, and returned with you. Well, Chaerephon, as you know, was very impetuous in all his doings, and he went to Delphi and boldly asked the oracle to tell him whether—as I was saying, I must beg you not to interrupt—he asked the oracle to tell him whether anyone was wiser than I was, and the Pythian prophetess answered, that there was no man wiser. Chaerephon is dead himself; but his brother, who is in court, will confirm the truth of what I am saying.

Why do I mention this? Because I am going to explain to you why I have such an evil name. When I heard the answer, I said to myself, 'What can the god mean? And what is the interpretation of his riddle? For I know that I have no wisdom, small or great. What then can he mean when he says that I am the wisest of men?' And yet he is a god, and cannot lie; that would be against his nature. After long consideration, I thought of a method of trying the question. I reflected that if I could only find a man wiser than myself, then I might go to the god with a refutation in my hand. I should say to him, 'Here is a man who is wiser than I am; but you said that I was the wisest.' Accordingly I went to one who had the reputation of wisdom, and observed him—his name I need not mention; he was a politician whom I selected for examination—and the result was as follows: When I began to talk with him, I could not help thinking that he was not really wise, although he was thought wise by many, and still wiser by himself; and thereupon I tried to explain to him that he thought himself wise, but was not really wise; and the consequence was that he hated me, and his enmity was shared by several who were present and heard me. So I left him, saying to myself, as I went away: Well, although I do not suppose that either of us knows anything really beautiful and good, I am better off than he is, for he knows nothing, and thinks that he knows; I neither know nor think that I know. In this latter particular, then, I seem to have slightly the advantage of him. Then I went to another who had still higher pretensions to wisdom, and my conclusion was exactly the same. Whereupon I made another enemy of him, and of many others besides him.

Then I went to one man after another, being not unconscious of the enmity which I provoked, and I lamented and feared this: but necessity was laid upon me—the word of God, I thought, ought to be considered first. And I said to myself, 'Go I must to all who appear to know, and find out the meaning of the oracle.' And I swear to you, Athenians, by the dog I swear!—for I must tell you the truth—the result of my mission was just this: I found that the men most in repute were all but the most foolish; and that others less esteemed were really wiser and better. I will tell you the tale of my wanderings and of the 'Herculean' labours, as I may call them, which I endured only to find at last the oracle irrefutable. After the politicians, I went to the poets; tragic, dithyrambic, and all sorts. And there, I said to myself, you will be instantly detected; now you will find out that you are more ignorant than they are. Accordingly, I took them some of the most elaborate passages in their own writings, and asked what was the meaning of them—thinking that they would teach me something. Will you believe me? I am almost ashamed to confess the truth, but I must say that there is hardly a person present who would not have talked better about their poetry than they did themselves. Then I knew that not by wisdom do poets write poetry, but by a sort of genius and inspiration; they are like diviners or soothsayers who also say many fine things, but do not understand the meaning of them. The poets appeared to me to be much in the same case; and I further observed that upon the strength of their poetry they believed themselves to be the wisest of men in other things in which they were not wise. So I departed, conceiving myself to be superior to them for the same reason that I was superior to the politicians.

At last I went to the artisans. I was conscious that I knew nothing at all, as I may say, and I was sure that they knew many fine things; and here I was not mistaken, for they did know many things of which I was ignorant, and in this they certainly were wiser than I was. But I observed that even the good artisans fell into the same error as the poets; because they were good workmen they thought that they also knew all sorts of high matters, and this defect in them overshadowed their wisdom; and therefore I asked myself on behalf of the oracle, whether I would like to be as I was, neither having their knowledge nor their ignorance, or like them in both; and I made answer to myself and to the oracle that I was better off as I was.

This inquisition has led to my having many enemies of the worst and most dangerous kind, and has given occasion also to many calumnies. And I am called wise, for my hearers always imagine that I myself possess the wisdom which I find wanting in others: but the truth is, O men of Athens, that God only is wise; and by his answer he intends to show that the wisdom of men is worth little or nothing; he is not speaking of Socrates, he is only using my name by way of illustration, as if he said, He, O men, is the wisest, who, like Socrates, knows that his wisdom is in truth worth nothing. And so I go about the world, obedient to the god, and search and make inquiry into the wisdom of any one, whether citizen or stranger, who appears to be wise; and if he is not wise, then in vindication of the oracle I show him that he is not wise; and my occupation quite absorbs me, and I have no time to give either to any public matter of interest or to any concern of my own, but I am in utter poverty by reason of my devotion to the god.

There is another thing: young men of the richer classes, who have not much to do, come about me of their own accord; they like to hear the pretenders examined, and they often imitate me, and proceed to examine others; there are plenty of persons, as they quickly discover, who think that they know something, but really know little or nothing; and then those who are examined by them instead of being angry with themselves are angry with me: This confounded Socrates, they say; this villainous misleader of youth! And then if somebody asks them, 'Why, what evil does he practise or teach?' They do not know, and cannot tell; but in order that they may not appear to be at a loss, they repeat the ready-made charges which are used against all philosophers about teaching things up in the clouds and under the earth, and having no gods, and making the worse appear the better cause; for they do not like to confess that their pretence of knowledge has been detected—which is the truth; and as they are numerous and ambitious and energetic, and are drawn up in battle array and have persuasive tongues, they have filled your ears with their loud and inveterate calumnies. And this is the reason why my three accusers, Meletus and Anytus and Lycon, have set upon me; Meletus, who has a quarrel with me on behalf of the poets; Anytus, on behalf of the craftsmen and politicians; Lycon, on behalf of the rhetoricians: and as I said at the beginning, I cannot expect to get rid of such a mass of calumny all in a moment. And this, O men of Athens, is the truth and the whole truth; I have concealed nothing, I have dissembled nothing. And yet, I know that my plainness of speech makes them hate me, and what is their hatred but a proof that I am speaking the truth? Hence has arisen the prejudice against me; and this is the reason of it, as you will find out either in this or in any future inquiry.

I have said enough in my defense against the first class of my accusers; I turn to the second class. They are headed by Meletus, that good man and true lover of his country, as he calls himself. Against these, too, I must try to make a defense—Let their affidavit be read: it contains something of this kind: It says that Socrates is a doer of evil, who corrupts the youth; and who does not believe in the gods of the state, but has other new divinities of his own. Such is the charge; and now let us examine the particular counts. He says that I am a doer of evil, and corrupt the youth; but I say, O men of Athens, that Meletus is a doer of evil, in that he pretends to be in earnest when he is only in jest, and is so eager to bring men to trial from a pretended zeal and interest about matters in which he really never had the smallest interest. And the truth of this I will endeavour to prove to you.

Come hither, Meletus, and let me ask a question of you. You think a great deal about the improvement of youth?

'Yes, I do.'

Tell the judges, then, who is their improver; for you must know, as you have taken the pains to discover their corrupter, and are citing and accusing me before them. Speak, then, and tell the judges who their improver is.... Observe, Meletus, that you are silent, and have nothing to say. But is not this rather disgraceful, and a very considerable proof of what I was saying, that you have no interest in the matter? Speak up, friend, and tell us who their improver is.

'The laws.'

But that, my good sir, is not my meaning. I want to know who the person is, who, in the first place, knows the laws.

'The judges, Socrates, who are present in court.'

What, do you mean to say, Meletus, that they are able to instruct and improve youth?

'Certainly they are.'

What, all of them, or some only and not others?

'All of them.'

By the goddess Hera, that is good news! There are plenty of improvers, then. And what do you say of the audience—do they improve them?

'Yes, they do.'

And the senators?

'Yes, the senators improve them.'

But perhaps the members of the assembly corrupt them?—or do they too improve them?

'They improve them.'

Then every Athenian improves and elevates them; all with the exception of myself; and I alone am their corrupter?

'Is that what you affirm? That is what I stoutly affirm.'

I am very unfortunate if you are right. But suppose I ask you a question: How about horses? Does one man do them harm and all the world good? Is not the exact opposite the truth? One man is able to do them good, or at least not many—the trainer of horses, that is to say, does them good, and others who have to do with them rather injure them? Is not that true, Meletus, of horses, or of any other animals? Most assuredly it is; whether you and Anytus say yes or no. Happy indeed would be the condition of youth if they had one corrupter only, and all the rest of the world were their improvers. But you, Meletus, have sufficiently shown that you never had a thought about the young: your carelessness is seen in your not caring about the very things which you bring against me.

And now, Meletus, I will ask you another question—by Zeus I will: Which is better, to live among bad citizens, or among good ones? Answer, friend, I say; the question is one which may be easily answered. Do not the good do their neighbours good, and the bad do them evil?

'Certainly.'

And is there anyone who would rather be injured than benefited by those who live with him? Answer, my good friend, the law requires you to answer—does anyone like to be injured?

'Certainly not.'

And when you accuse me of corrupting and deteriorating the youth, do you allege that I corrupt them intentionally or unintentionally?

'Intentionally, I say.'

But you have just admitted that the good do their neighbours good, and the evil do them evil. Now, is that a truth which your superior wisdom has recognized thus early in life, and am I, at my age, in such darkness and ignorance as not to know that if a man with whom I have to live is corrupted by me, I am very likely to be harmed by him; and yet I corrupt him, and intentionally, too—so you say, although neither I nor any other human being is ever likely to be convinced by you. But either I do not corrupt them, or I corrupt them unintentionally; and on either view of the case you lie. If my offence is unintentional, the law has no cognizance of unintentional offences: you ought to have taken me privately, and warned and admonished me; for if I had been better advised, I should have left off doing what I only did unintentionally—no doubt I should; but you would have nothing to say to me and refused to teach me. And now you bring me up in this court, which is a place not of instruction, but of punishment.

It will be very clear to you, Athenians, as I was saying, that Meletus has no care at all, great or small, about the matter. But still I should like to know, Meletus, in what I am affirmed to corrupt the young. I suppose you mean, as I infer from your indictment, that I teach them not to acknowledge the gods which the state acknowledges, but some other new divinities or spiritual agencies in their stead. These are the lessons by which I corrupt the youth, as you say.

'Yes, that I say emphatically.'

Then, by the gods, Meletus, of whom we are speaking, tell me and the court, in somewhat plainer terms, what you mean! For I do not as yet understand whether you affirm that I teach other men to acknowledge some gods, and therefore that I do believe in gods, and am not an entire atheist—this you do not lay to my charge,—but only you say that they are not the same gods which the city recognizes—the charge is that they are different gods. Or, do you mean that I am an atheist simply, and a teacher of atheism?

'I mean the latter—that you are a complete atheist.'

What an extraordinary statement! Why do you think so, Meletus? Do you mean that I do not believe in the godhead of the sun or moon, like other men?

'I assure you, judges, that he does not: for he says that the sun is stone, and the moon earth.'

Friend Meletus, you think that you are accusing Anaxagoras: and you have but a bad opinion of the judges, if you fancy them illiterate to such a degree as not to know that these doctrines are found in the books of Anaxagoras the Clazomenian, which are full of them. And so, forsooth, the youth are said to be taught them by Socrates, when there are not unfrequently exhibitions of them at the theatre† (price of admission one drachma at the most); and they might pay their money, and laugh at Socrates if he pretends to father these extraordinary views. And so, Meletus, you really think that I do not believe in any god?

'I swear by Zeus that you believe absolutely in none at all.'

Nobody will believe you, Meletus, and I am pretty sure that you do not believe yourself. I cannot help thinking, men of Athens, that Meletus is reckless and impudent, and that he has written this indictment in a spirit of mere wantonness and youthful bravado. Has he not compounded a riddle, thinking to try me? He said to himself: I shall see whether the wise Socrates will discover my facetious contradiction, or whether I shall be able to deceive him and the rest of them. For he certainly does appear to me to contradict himself in the indictment as much as if he said that Socrates is guilty of not believing in the gods, and yet of believing in them—but this is not like a person who is in earnest.

I should like you, O men of Athens, to join me in examining what I conceive to be his inconsistency; and do you, Meletus, answer. And I must remind the audience of my request that they would not make a disturbance if I speak in my accustomed manner: Did ever man, Meletus, believe in the existence of human things, and not of human beings?...I wish, men of Athens, that he would answer, and not be always trying to get up an interruption.

Did ever any man believe in horsemanship, and not in horses? or in flute-playing, and not in flute-players? No, my friend; I will answer to you and to the court, as you refuse to answer for yourself.

---

†Probably in allusion to Aristophanes who caricatured, and to Euripides who borrowed the notions of Anaxagoras, as well as to other dramatic poets.

APOLOGY

There is no man who ever did. But now please to answer the next question: Can a man believe in spiritual and divine agencies, and not in spirits or demigods?

'He cannot.'

How lucky I am to have extracted that answer, by the assistance of the court! But then you swear in the indictment that I teach and believe in divine or spiritual agencies (new or old, no matter for that); at any rate, I believe in spiritual agencies,—so you say and swear in the affidavit; and yet if I believe in divine beings, how can I help believing in spirits or demigods;—must I not? To be sure I must; and therefore I may assume that your silence gives consent. Now what are spirits or demigods? Are they not either gods or the sons of gods?

'Certainly they are.'

But this is what I call the facetious riddle invented by you: the demigods or spirits are gods, and you say first that I do not believe in gods, and then again that I do believe in gods; that is, if I believe in demigods. For if the demigods are the illegitimate sons of gods, whether by the nymphs or by any other mothers, of whom they are said to be the sons—what human being will ever believe that there are no gods if they are the sons of gods? You might as well affirm the existence of mules, and deny that of horses and asses. Such nonsense, Meletus, could only have been intended by you to make trial of me. You have put this into the indictment because you had nothing real of which to accuse me. But no one who has a particle of understanding will ever be convinced by you that the same men can believe in divine and superhuman things, and yet not believe that there are gods and demigods and heroes.

I have said enough in answer to the charge of Meletus: any elaborate defense is unnecessary, but I know only too well how many are the enmities which I have incurred, and this is what will be my destruction if I am destroyed; not Meletus, nor yet Anytus, but the envy and detraction of the world, which has been the death of many good men, and will probably be the death of many more; there is no danger of my being the last of them.

Someone will say: 'And are you not ashamed, Socrates, of a course of life which is likely to bring you to an untimely end?' To him I may fairly answer: There you are mistaken: a man who is good for anything ought not to calculate the chance of living or dying; he ought only to consider whether in doing anything he is doing right or wrong—acting the part of a good man or of a bad. Whereas, upon your view, the heroes who fell at Troy were not good for much, and the son of Thetis above all, who altogether despised danger in comparison with disgrace; and when he was so eager to slay Hector, his goddess mother said to him, that if he avenged his companion Patroclus, and slew Hector, he would die himself—'Fate,' she said, in these or the like words, 'waits for you next after Hector;' he, receiving this warning, utterly despised danger and death, and instead of fearing them, feared rather to live in dishonour, and not to avenge his friend. 'Let me die forthwith,' he replies, 'and be avenged of my enemy, rather than abide here by the beaked ships, a laughing-stock and a burden of the earth.' Had Achilles any thought of death and danger? For wherever a man's place is, whether the place which he has chosen or that in which he has been placed by a commander, there he ought to remain in the hour of danger; he should not think of death or of anything but of disgrace. And this, O men of Athens, is a true saying.

APOLOGY

Strange, indeed, would be my conduct, O men of Athens, if I who, when I was ordered by the generals whom you chose to command me at Potidaea and Amphipolis and Delium, remained where they placed me, like any other man, facing death—if now, when, as I conceive and imagine, God orders me to fulfilll the philosopher's mission of searching into myself and other men, I were to desert my post through fear of death, or any other fear; that would indeed be strange, and I might justly be arraigned in court for denying the existence of the gods, if I disobeyed the oracle because I was afraid of death, fancying that I was wise when I was not wise. For the fear of death is indeed the pretence of wisdom, and not real wisdom, being a pretence of knowing the unknown; and no one knows whether death, which men in their fear apprehend to be the greatest evil, may not be the greatest good. Is not this ignorance of a disgraceful sort, the ignorance which is the conceit that a man knows what he does not know? And in this respect only I believe myself to differ from men in general, and may perhaps claim to be wiser than they are: that whereas I know but little of the world below, I do not suppose that I know: but I do know that injustice and disobedience to a better, whether God or man, is evil and dishonourable, and I will never fear or avoid a possible good rather than a certain evil. And therefore if you let me go now, and are not convinced by Anytus, who said that since I had been prosecuted I must be put to death; (or if not that I ought never to have been prosecuted at all); and that if I escape now, your sons will all be utterly ruined by listening to my words—if you say to me, Socrates, this time we will not mind Anytus, and you shall be let off, but upon one condition, that you are not to inquire and speculate in this way any more, and that if you are caught doing so again you shall die; if this was the condition on which you let me go, I should reply: Men of Athens, I honour and love you; but I shall obey God rather than you, and while I have life and strength I shall never cease from the practice and teaching of philosophy, exhorting any one whom I meet and saying to him after my manner: You, my friend, a citizen of the great and mighty and wise city of Athens, are you not ashamed of heaping up the greatest amount of money and honour and reputation, and caring so little about wisdom and truth and the greatest improvement of the soul, which you never regard or heed at all? And if the person with whom I am arguing, says: Yes, but I do care; then I do not leave him or let him go at once; but I proceed to interrogate and examine and cross-examine him, and if I think that he has no virtue in him, but only says that he has, I reproach him with undervaluing the greater, and overvaluing the less. And I shall repeat the same words to every one whom I meet, young and old, citizen and alien, but especially to the citizens, inasmuch as they are my brethren. For know that this is the command of God; and I believe that no greater good has ever happened in the state than my service to the God. For I do nothing but go about persuading you all, old and young alike, not to take thought for your persons or your properties, but first and chiefly to care about the greatest improvement of the soul. I tell you that virtue is not given by money, but that from virtue comes money and every other good of man, public as well as private. This is my teaching, and if this is the doctrine which corrupts the youth, I am a mischievous person. But if anyone says that this is not my teaching, he is speaking an untruth. Wherefore, O men of Athens, I say to you, do as Anytus bids or not as Anytus bids, and either acquit me or not; but whichever you do, understand that I shall never alter my ways, not even if I have to die many times.

Men of Athens, do not interrupt, but hear me; there was an understanding between us that you should hear me to the end: I have something more to say, at which you may be inclined to cry out; but I believe that to hear me will be good for you, and therefore I beg that you will not cry out. I would have you know, that if you kill such an one as I am, you will injure yourselves more than you will injure me. Nothing will injure me, not Meletus nor yet Anytus—they cannot, for a bad man is not permitted to injure a better than himself. I do not deny that Anytus may, perhaps, kill him, or drive him into exile, or deprive him of civil rights; and he may imagine, and others may imagine, that he is inflicting a great injury upon him: but there I do not agree. For the evil of doing as he is doing—the evil of unjustly taking away the life of another—is greater far.

And now, Athenians, I am not going to argue for my own sake, as you may think, but for yours, that you may not sin against the God by condemning me, who am his gift to you. For if you kill me you will not easily find a successor to me, who, if I may use such a ludicrous figure of speech, am a sort of gadfly, given to the state by God; and the state is a great and noble steed who is tardy in his motions owing to his very size, and requires to be stirred into life. I am that gadfly which God has attached to the state, and all day long and in all places am always fastening upon you, arousing and persuading and reproaching you. You will not easily find another like me, and therefore I would advise you to spare me. I dare say that you may feel out of temper (like a person who is suddenly awakened from sleep), and you think that you might easily strike me dead as Anytus advises, and then you would sleep on for the remainder of your lives, unless God in his care of you sent you another gadfly. When I say that I am given to you by God, the proof of my mission is this: if I had been like other men, I should not have neglected all my own concerns or patiently seen the neglect of them during all these years, and have been doing yours, coming to you individually like a father or elder brother, exhorting you to regard virtue; such conduct, I say, would be unlike human nature. If I had gained anything, or if my exhortations had been paid, there would have been some sense in my doing so; but now, as you will perceive, not even the impudence of my accusers dares to say that I have ever exacted or sought pay of any one; of that they have no witness. And I have a sufficient witness to the truth of what I say—my poverty.

Someone may wonder why I go about in private giving advice and busying myself with the concerns of others, but do not venture to come forward in public and advise the state. I will tell you why. You have heard me speak at sundry times and in divers places of an oracle or sign which comes to me, and is the divinity which Meletus ridicules in the indictment. This sign, which is a kind of voice, first began to come to me when I was a child; it always forbids but never commands me to do anything which I am going to do. This is what deters me from being a politician. And rightly, as I think. For I am certain, O men of Athens, that if I had engaged in politics, I should have perished long ago, and done no good either to you or to myself. And do not be offended at my telling you the truth: for the truth is, that no man who goes to war with you or any other multitude, honestly striving against the many lawless and unrighteous deeds which are done in a state, will save his life; he who will fight for the right, if he would live even for a brief space, must have a private station and not a public one.

I can give you convincing evidence of what I say, not words only, but what you value far more—actions. Let me relate to you a passage of my own life which will prove to you that I should never have yielded to injustice from any fear of death, and that 'as I should have refused to yield' I must have died at once. I will tell you a tale of the courts, not very interesting perhaps, but nevertheless true. The only office of state which I ever held, O men of Athens, was that of senator: the tribe Antiochis, which is my tribe, had the presidency at the trial of the generals who had not taken up the bodies of the slain after the battle of Arginusae; and you proposed to try them in a body, contrary to law, as you all thought afterwards; but at the time I was the only one of the Prytanes who was opposed to the illegality, and I gave my vote against you; and when the orators threatened to impeach and arrest me, and you called and shouted, I made up my mind that I would run the risk, having law and justice with me, rather than take part in your injustice because I feared imprisonment and death. This happened in the days of the democracy. But when the oligarchy of the Thirty was in power, they sent for me and four others into the rotunda, and bade us bring Leon the Salaminian from Salamis, as they wanted to put him to death. This was a specimen of the sort of commands which they were always giving with the view of implicating as many as possible in their crimes; and then I showed, not in word only but in deed, that, if I may be allowed to use such an expression, I cared not a straw for death, and that my great and only care was lest I should do an unrighteous or unholy thing. For the strong arm of that oppressive power did not frighten me into doing wrong; and when we came out of the rotunda the other four went to Salamis and fetched Leon, but I went quietly home. For which I might have lost my life, had not the power of the Thirty shortly afterwards come to an end. And many will witness to my words.

Now do you really imagine that I could have survived all these years, if I had led a public life, supposing that like a good man I had always maintained the right and had made justice, as I ought, the first thing? No indeed, men of Athens, neither I nor any other man. But I have been always the same in all my actions, public as well as private, and never have I yielded any base compliance to those who are slanderously termed my disciples, or to any other. Not that I have any regular disciples. But if any one likes to come and hear me while I am pursuing my mission, whether he be young or old, he is not excluded. Nor do I converse only with those who pay; but any one, whether he be rich or poor, may ask and answer me and listen to my words; and whether he turns out to be a bad man or a good one, neither result can be justly imputed to me; for I never taught or professed to teach him anything. And if anyone says that he has ever learned or heard anything from me in private which all the world has not heard, let me tell you that he is lying.

But I shall be asked, 'Why do people delight in continually conversing with you?' I have told you already, Athenians, the whole truth about this matter: they like to hear the cross-examination of the pretenders to wisdom; there is amusement in it. Now this duty of cross-examining other men has been imposed upon me by God; and has been signified to me by oracles, visions, and in every way in which the will of divine power was ever intimated to anyone. This is true, O Athenians, or, if not true, would be soon refuted. If I am or have been corrupting the youth, those of them who are now grown up and have become sensible that I gave them bad advice in the days of their youth should come forward as accusers, and take their revenge; or if they do not like to come themselves, some of their relatives, fathers, brothers, or other kinsmen, should say what evil their families have suffered at my hands. Now is their time. Many of them I see in the court. There is Crito, who is of the same age and of the same deme with myself, and there is Critobulus his son, whom I also see. Then again there is Lysanias of Sphettus, who is the father of Aeschines—he is present; and also there is Antiphon of Cephisus, who is the father of Epigenes; and there are the brothers of several who have associated with me. There is Nicostratus the son of Theosdotides, and the brother of Theodotus (now Theodotus himself is dead, and therefore he, at any rate, will not seek to stop him); and there is Paralus the son of Demodocus, who had a brother Theages; and Adeimantus the son of Ariston, whose brother Plato is present; and Aeantodorus, who is the brother of Apollodorus, whom I also see. I might mention a great many others, some of whom Meletus should have produced as witnesses in the course of his speech; and let him still produce them, if he has forgotten—I will make way for him. And let him say, if he has any testimony of the sort which he can produce. Nay, Athenians, the very opposite is the truth. For all these are ready to witness on behalf of the corrupter, of the injurer of their kindred, as Meletus and Anytus call me; not the corrupted youth only—there might have been a motive for that—but their uncorrupted elder relatives. Why should they too support me with their testimony? Why, indeed, except for the sake of truth and justice, and because they know that I am speaking the truth, and that Meletus is a liar.

Well, Athenians, this and the like of this is all the defense which I have to offer. Yet a word more. Perhaps there may be someone who is offended at me, when he calls to mind how he himself on a similar, or even a less serious occasion, prayed and entreated the judges with many tears, and how he produced his children in court, which was a moving spectacle, together with a host of relations and friends; whereas I, who am probably in danger of my life, will do none of these things. The contrast may occur to his mind, and he may be set against me, and vote in anger because he is displeased at me on this account. Now if there be such a person among you,—mind, I do not say that there is,—to him I may fairly reply: My friend, I am a man, and like other men, a creature of flesh and blood, and not 'of wood or stone,' as Homer says; and I have a family, yes, and sons,

O Athenians, three in number, one almost a man, and two others who are still young; and yet I will not bring any of them hither in order to petition you for an acquittal. And why not? Not from any self-assertion or want of respect for you. Whether I am or am not afraid of death is another question, of which I will not now speak. But, having regard to public opinion, I feel that such conduct would be discreditable to myself, and to you, and to the whole state. One who has reached my years, and who has a name for wisdom, ought not to demean himself. Whether this opinion of me be deserved or not, at any rate the world has decided that Socrates is in some way superior to other men. And if those among you who are said to be superior in wisdom and courage, and any other virtue, demean themselves in this way, how shameful is their conduct! I have seen men of reputation, when they have been condemned, behaving in the strangest manner: they seemed to fancy that they were going to suffer something dreadful if they died, and that they could be immortal if you only allowed them to live; and I think that such are a dishonour to the state, and that any stranger coming in would have said of them that the most eminent men of Athens, to whom the Athenians themselves give honour and command, are no better than women. And I say that these things ought not to be done by those of us who have a reputation; and if they are done, you ought not to permit them; you ought rather to show that you are far more disposed to condemn the man who gets up a doleful scene and makes the city ridiculous, than him who holds his peace.

But, setting aside the question of public opinion, there seems to be something wrong in asking a favour of a judge, and thus procuring an acquittal, instead of informing and convincing him. For his duty is, not to make a present of justice, but to give judgment; and he has sworn that he will judge according to the laws, and not according to his own good pleasure; and we ought not to encourage you, nor should you allow yourselves to be encouraged, in this habit of perjury—there can be no piety in that. Do not then require me to do what I consider dishonourable and impious and wrong, especially now, when I am being tried for impiety on the indictment of Meletus. For if, O men of Athens, by force of persuasion and entreaty I could overpower your oaths, then I should be teaching you to believe that there are no gods, and in defending should simply convict myself of the charge of not believing in them. But that is not so—far otherwise. For I do believe that there are gods, and in a sense higher than that in which any of my accusers believe in them. And to you and to God I commit my cause, to be determined by you as is best for you and me.

...

There are many reasons why I am not grieved, O men of Athens, at the vote of condemnation. I expected it, and am only surprised that the votes are so nearly equal; for I had thought that the majority against me would have been far larger; but now, had thirty votes gone over to the other side, I should have been acquitted. And I may say, I think, that I have escaped Meletus. I may say more; for without the assistance of Anytus and Lycon, any one may see that he would not have had a fifth part of the votes, as the law requires, in which case he would have incurred a fine of a thousand drachmae.

And so he proposes death as the penalty. And what shall I propose on my part, O men of Athens? Clearly that which is my due. And what is my due? What return shall be made to the man who has never had the wit to be idle during his whole life; but has been careless of what the many care for—wealth, and family interests, and military offices, and speaking in the assembly, and magistracies, and plots, and parties. Reflecting that I was really too honest a man to be a politician and live, I did not go where I could do no good to you or to myself; but where I could do the greatest good privately to every one of you, thither I went, and sought to persuade every man among you that he must look to himself, and seek virtue and wisdom before he looks to his private interests, and look to the state before he looks to the interests of the state; and that this should be the order which he observes in all his actions. What shall be done to such a one? Doubtless some good thing, O men of Athens, if he has his reward; and the good should be of a kind suitable to him. What would be a reward suitable to a poor man who is your benefactor, and who desires leisure that he may instruct you? There can be no reward so fitting as maintenance in the Prytaneum, O men of Athens, a reward which he deserves far more than the citizen who has won the prize at Olympia in the horse or chariot race, whether the chariots were drawn by two horses or by many. For I am in want, and he has enough; and he only gives you the appearance of happiness, and I give you the reality. And if I am to estimate the penalty fairly, I should say that maintenance in the Prytaneum is the just return.

Perhaps you think that I am braving you in what I am saying now, as in what I said before about the tears and prayers. But this is not so. I speak rather because I am convinced that I never intentionally wronged any one, although I cannot convince you—the time has been too short; if there were a law at Athens, as there is in other cities, that a capital cause should not be decided in one day, then I believe that I should have convinced you. But I cannot in a moment refute great slanders; and, as I am convinced that I never wronged another, I will assuredly not wrong myself. I will not say of myself that I deserve any evil, or propose any penalty. Why should

I? Because I am afraid of the penalty of death which Meletus proposes? When I do not know whether death is a good or an evil, why should I propose a penalty which would certainly be an evil? Shall I say imprisonment? And why should I live in prison, and be the slave of the magistrates of the year—of the Eleven? Or shall the penalty be a fine, and imprisonment until the fine is paid? There is the same objection. I should have to lie in prison, for money I have none, and cannot pay. And if I say exile (and this may possibly be the penalty which you will affix), I must indeed be blinded by the love of life, if I am so irrational as to expect that when you, who are my own citizens, cannot endure my discourses and words, and have found them so grievous and odious that you will have no more of them, others are likely to endure me. No indeed, men of Athens, that is not very likely. And what a life should I lead, at my age, wandering from city to city, ever changing my place of exile, and always being driven out! For I am quite sure that wherever I go, there, as here, the young men will flock to me; and if I drive them away, their elders will drive me out at their request; and if I let them come, their fathers and friends will drive me out for their sakes.

Someone will say: Yes, Socrates, but cannot you hold your tongue, and then you may go into a foreign city, and no one will interfere with you? Now I have great difficulty in making you understand my answer to this. For if I tell you that to do as you say would be a disobedience to the God, and therefore that I cannot hold my tongue, you will not believe that I am serious; and if I say again that daily to discourse about virtue, and of those other things about which you hear me examining myself and others, is the greatest good of man, and that the unexamined life is not worth living, you are still less likely to believe me. Yet I say what is true, although a thing of which it is hard for me to persuade you. Also, I have never been accustomed to think that I deserve to suffer any harm. Had I money I might have estimated the offence at what I was able to pay, and not have been much the worse. But I have none, and therefore I must ask you to proportion the fine to my means. Well, perhaps I could afford a mina, and therefore I propose that penalty: Plato, Crito, Critobulus, and Apollodorus, my friends here, bid me say thirty minae, and they will be the sureties. Let thirty minae be the penalty; for which sum they will be ample security to you.

...

Not much time will be gained, O Athenians, in return for the evil name which you will get from the detractors of the city, who will say that you killed Socrates, a wise man; for they will call me wise, even although I am not wise, when they want to reproach you. If you had waited a little while, your desire would have been fulfillled in the course of nature. For I am far advanced in years, as you may perceive, and not far from death. I am speaking now not to all of you, but only to those who have condemned me to death. And I have another thing to say to them: you think that I was convicted because I had no words of the sort which would have procured my acquittal—I mean, if I had thought fit to leave nothing undone or unsaid. Not so; the deficiency which led to my conviction was not of words—certainly not. But I had not the boldness or impudence or inclination to address you as you would have liked me to do, weeping and wailing and lamenting, and saying and doing many things which you have been accustomed to hear from others, and which, as I maintain, are unworthy of me. I thought at the time that I ought not to do anything common or mean when in danger: nor do I now repent of the style of my defense; I would rather die having spoken after my manner, than speak in your manner and live. For neither in war nor yet at law ought I or any man to use every way of escaping death. Often in battle there can be no doubt that if a man will throw away his arms, and fall on his knees before his pursuers, he may escape death; and in other dangers there are other ways of escaping death, if a man is willing to say and do anything. The difficulty, my friends, is not to avoid death, but to avoid unrighteousness; for that runs faster than death. I am old and move slowly, and the slower runner has overtaken me, and my accusers are keen and quick, and the faster runner, who is unrighteousness, has overtaken them. And now I depart hence condemned by you to suffer the penalty of death,—they too go their ways condemned by the truth to suffer the penalty of villainy and wrong; and I must abide by my award—let them abide by theirs. I suppose that these things may be regarded as fated,—and I think that they are well.

And now, O men who have condemned me, I would fain prophesy to you; for I am about to die, and in the hour of death men are gifted with prophetic power. And I prophesy to you who are my murderers, that immediately after my departure punishment far heavier than you have inflicted on me will surely await you. Me you have killed because you wanted to escape the accuser, and not to give an account of your lives. But that will not be as you suppose: far otherwise. For I say that there will be more accusers of you than there are now; accusers whom hitherto I have restrained: and as they are younger they will be more inconsiderate with you, and you will be more offended at them. If you think that by killing men you can prevent someone from censuring your evil lives, you are mistaken; that is not a way of escape which is either possible or honourable; the easiest and the noblest way is not to be disabling others, but to be improving yourselves. This is the prophecy which I utter before my departure to the judges who have condemned me.

Friends, who would have acquitted me, I would like also to talk with you about the thing which has come to pass, while the magistrates are busy, and before I go to the place at which I must die. Stay then a little, for we may as well talk with one another while there is time. You are my friends, and I should like to show you the meaning of this event which has happened to me. O my judges—for you I may truly call judges—I should like to tell you of a wonderful circumstance. Hitherto the divine faculty of which the internal oracle is the source has constantly been in the habit of opposing me even about trifles, if I was going to make a slip or error in any matter; and now as you see there has come upon me that which may be thought, and is generally believed to be, the last and worst evil. But the oracle made no sign of opposition, either when I was leaving my house in the morning, or when I was on my way to the court, or while I was speaking, at anything which I was going to say; and yet I have often been stopped in the middle of a speech, but now in nothing I either said or did touching the matter in hand has the oracle opposed me. What do I take to be the explanation of this silence? I will tell you. It is an intimation that what has happened to me is a good, and that those of us who think that death is an evil are in error. For the customary sign would surely have opposed me had I been going to evil and not to good.

Let us reflect in another way, and we shall see that there is great reason to hope that death is a good; for one of two things—either death is a state of nothingness and utter unconsciousness, or, as men say, there is a change and migration of the soul from this world to another. Now if you suppose that there is no consciousness, but a sleep like the sleep of him who is undisturbed even by dreams, death will be an unspeakable gain. For if a person were to select the night in which his sleep was undisturbed even by dreams, and were to compare with this the other days and nights of his life, and then were to tell us how many days and nights he had passed in the course of his life better and more pleasantly than this one, I think that any man, I will not say a private man, but even the great king will not find many such days or nights, when compared with the others. Now if death be of such a nature, I say that to die is gain; for eternity is then only a single night. But if death is the journey to another place, and there, as men say, all the dead abide, what good, O my friends and judges, can be greater than this? If indeed when the pilgrim arrives in the world below, he is delivered from the professors of justice in this world, and finds the true judges who are said to give judgment there, Minos and Rhadamanthus and Aeacus and Triptolemus, and other sons of God who were righteous in their own life, that pilgrimage will be worth making. What would not a man give if he might converse with Orpheus and Musaeus and Hesiod and Homer? Nay, if this be true, let me die again and again. I myself, too, shall have a wonderful interest in there meeting and conversing with Palamedes, and Ajax the son of Telamon, and any other ancient hero who has suffered death through an unjust judgment; and there will be no small pleasure, as I think, in comparing my own sufferings with theirs. Above all, I shall then be able to continue my search into true and false knowledge; as in this world, so also in the next; and I shall find out who is wise, and who pretends to be wise, and is not. What would not a man give, O judges, to be able to examine the leader of the great Trojan expedition; or Odysseus or Sisyphus, or numberless others, men and women too! What infinite delight would there be in conversing with them and asking them questions! In another world they do not put a man to death for asking questions: assuredly not. For besides being happier than we are, they will be immortal, if what is said is true.

Wherefore, O judges, be of good cheer about death, and know of a certainty, that no evil can happen to a good man, either in life or after death. He and his are not neglected by the gods; nor has my own approaching end happened by mere chance. But I see clearly that the time had arrived when it was better for me to die and be released from trouble; wherefore the oracle gave no sign. For which reason, also, I am not angry with my condemners, or with my accusers; they have done me no harm, although they did not mean to do me any good; and for this I may gently blame them.

Still I have a favour to ask of them. When my sons are grown up, I would ask you, O my friends, to punish them; and I would have you trouble them, as I have troubled you, if they seem to care about riches, or anything, more than about virtue; or if they pretend to be something when they are really nothing,—then reprove them, as I have reproved you, for not caring about that for which they ought to care, and thinking that they are something when they are really nothing. And if you do this, both I and my sons will have received justice at your hands.

The hour of departure has arrived, and we go our ways—I to die, and you to live. Which is better God only knows.

CRITO

PERSONS OF THE DIALOGUE: Socrates, Crito.
SCENE: The Prison of Socrates.

SOCRATES: Why have you come at this hour, Crito? It must be quite early.

CRITO: Yes, certainly.

SOCRATES: What is the exact time?

CRITO: The dawn is breaking.

SOCRATES: I wonder that the keeper of the prison would let you in.

CRITO: He knows me because I often come, Socrates; moreover, I have done him a kindness.

SOCRATES: And are you only just arrived?

CRITO: No, I came some time ago.

SOCRATES: Then why did you sit and say nothing, instead of at once awakening me?

CRITO: I should not have liked myself, Socrates, to be in such great trouble and unrest as you are—indeed I should not: I have been watching with amazement your peaceful slumbers; and for that reason I did not awake you, because I wished to minimize the pain. I have always thought you to be of a happy disposition; but never did I see anything like the easy, tranquil manner in which you bear this calamity.

SOCRATES: Why, Crito, when a man has reached my age he ought not to be repining at the approach of death.

CRITO: And yet other old men find themselves in similar misfortunes, and age does not prevent them from repining.

SOCRATES: That is true. But you have not told me why you come at this early hour.

CRITO: I come to bring you a message which is sad and painful; not, as I believe, to yourself, but to all of us who are your friends, and saddest of all to me.

SOCRATES: What? Has the ship come from Delos, on the arrival of which I am to die?

CRITO: No, the ship has not actually arrived, but she will probably be here to-day, as persons who have come from Sunium tell me that they have left her there; and therefore to-morrow, Socrates, will be the last day of your life.

SOCRATES: Very well, Crito; if such is the will of God, I am willing; but my belief is that there will be a delay of a day.

CRITO: Why do you think so?

SOCRATES: I will tell you. I am to die on the day after the arrival of the ship?

CRITO: Yes; that is what the authorities say.

SOCRATES: But I do not think that the ship will be here until to-morrow; this I infer from a vision which I had last night, or rather only just now, when you fortunately allowed me to sleep.

CRITO: And what was the nature of the vision?

SOCRATES: There appeared to me the likeness of a woman, fair and comely, clothed in bright raiment, who called to me and said: O Socrates, 'The third day hence to fertile Phthia shalt thou go.'[†]

CRITO: What a singular dream, Socrates!

SOCRATES: There can be no doubt about the meaning, Crito, I think.

CRITO: Yes; the meaning is only too clear. But, oh! my beloved Socrates, let me entreat you once more to take my advice and escape. For if you die I shall not only lose a friend who can never be replaced, but there is another evil: people who do not know you and me will believe that I might have saved you if I had been willing to give money, but that I did not care. Now, can there be a worse disgrace than this—that I should be thought to value money more than the life of a friend? For the many will not be persuaded that I wanted you to escape, and that you refused.

SOCRATES: But why, my dear Crito, should we care about the opinion of the many? Good men, and they are

---

[†]Homer, Il.

the only persons who are worth considering, will think of these things truly as they occurred.

CRITO: But you see, Socrates, that the opinion of the many must be regarded, for what is now happening shows that they can do the greatest evil to anyone who has lost their good opinion.

SOCRATES: I only wish it were so, Crito; and that the many could do the greatest evil; for then they would also be able to do the greatest good—and what a fine thing this would be! But in reality they can do neither; for they cannot make a man either wise or foolish; and whatever they do is the result of chance.

CRITO: Well, I will not dispute with you; but please to tell me, Socrates, whether you are not acting out of regard to me and your other friends: are you not afraid that if you escape from prison we may get into trouble with the informers for having stolen you away, and lose either the whole or a great part of our property; or that even a worse evil may happen to us? Now, if you fear on our account, be at ease; for in order to save you, we ought surely to run this, or even a greater risk; be persuaded, then, and do as I say.

SOCRATES: Yes, Crito, that is one fear which you mention, but by no means the only one.

CRITO: Fear not—there are persons who are willing to get you out of prison at no great cost; and as for the informers they are far from being exorbitant in their demands—a little money will satisfy them. My means, which are certainly ample, are at your service, and if you have a scruple about spending all mine, here are strangers who will give you the use of theirs; and one of them, Simmias the Theban, has brought a large sum of money for this very purpose; and Cebes and many others are prepared to spend their money in helping you to escape. I say, therefore, do not hesitate on our account, and do not say, as you did in the court[†], that you will have a difficulty in knowing what to do with yourself anywhere else. For men will love you in other places to which you may go, and not in Athens only; there are friends of mine in Thessaly, if you like to go to them, who will value and protect you, and no Thessalian will give you any trouble. Nor can I think that you are at all justified, Socrates, in betraying your own life when you might be saved; in acting thus you are playing into the hands of your enemies, who are hurrying on your destruction. And further I should say that you are deserting your own children; for you might bring them up and educate them; instead of which you go away and leave them, and they will have to take their chance; and if they do not meet with the usual fate of orphans, there will be small thanks to you. No man should bring children into the world who is unwilling to persevere to the end in their nurture and education. But you appear to be choosing the easier part, not the better and manlier, which would have been more becoming in one who professes to care for virtue in all his actions, like yourself. And indeed, I am ashamed not only of you, but of us who are your friends, when I reflect that the whole business will be attributed entirely to our want of courage. The trial need never have come on, or might

[†]compare Apol.

have been managed differently; and this last act, or crowning folly, will seem to have occurred through our negligence and cowardice, who might have saved you, if we had been good for anything; and you might have saved yourself, for there was no difficulty at all. See now, Socrates, how sad and discreditable are the consequences, both to us and you. Make up your mind then, or rather have your mind already made up, for the time of deliberation is over, and there is only one thing to be done, which must be done this very night, and if we delay at all will be no longer practicable or possible; I beseech you therefore, Socrates, be persuaded by me, and do as I say.

SOCRATES: Dear Crito, your zeal is invaluable, if a right one; but if wrong, the greater the zeal the greater the danger; and therefore we ought to consider whether I shall or shall not do as you say. For I am and always have been one of those natures who must be guided by reason, whatever the reason may be which upon reflection appears to me to be the best; and now that this chance has befallen me, I cannot repudiate my own words: the principles which I have hitherto honoured and revered I still honour, and unless we can at once find other and better principles, I am certain not to agree with you; no, not even if the power of the multitude could inflict many more imprisonments, confiscations, deaths, frightening us like children with hobgoblin terrors[†]. What will be the fairest way of considering the question? Shall I return to your old argument about the opinions of men?—we were saying that some of

---

[†]compare Apol.

them are to be regarded, and others not. Now were we right in maintaining this before I was condemned? And has the argument which was once good now proved to be talk for the sake of talking—mere childish nonsense? That is what I want to consider with your help—whether, under my present circumstances, the argument appears to be in any way different or not; and is to be allowed by me or disallowed. That argument, which, as I believe, is maintained by many persons of authority, was to the effect, as I was saying, that the opinions of some men are to be regarded, and of other men not to be regarded. Now you, Crito, are not going to die to-morrow—at least, there is no human probability of this, and therefore you are disinterested and not liable to be deceived by the circumstances in which you are placed. Tell me then, whether I am right in saying that some opinions, and the opinions of some men only, are to be valued, and that other opinions, and the opinions of other men, are not to be valued. I ask you whether I was right in maintaining this?

CRITO: Certainly.

SOCRATES: The good are to be regarded, and not the bad?

CRITO: Yes.

SOCRATES: And the opinions of the wise are good, and the opinions of the unwise are evil?

CRITO: Certainly.

SOCRATES: And what was said about another matter? Is the pupil who devotes himself to the practice of gymnastics supposed to attend to the praise and blame and opinion of every man, or of one man only—his physician or trainer, whoever he may be?

CRITO: Of one man only.

SOCRATES: And he ought to fear the censure and welcome the praise of that one only, and not of the many?

CRITO: Clearly so.

SOCRATES: And he ought to act and train, and eat and drink in the way which seems good to his single master who has understanding, rather than according to the opinion of all other men put together?

CRITO: True.

SOCRATES: And if he disobeys and disregards the opinion and approval of the one, and regards the opinion of the many who have no understanding, will he not suffer evil?

CRITO: Certainly he will.

SOCRATES: And what will the evil be, whither tending and what affecting, in the disobedient person?

CRITO: Clearly, affecting the body; that is what is destroyed by the evil.

SOCRATES: Very good; and is not this true, Crito, of other things which we need not separately enumerate? In questions of just and unjust, fair and foul, good and evil, which are the subjects of our present consultation, ought we to follow the opinion of the many and to fear them; or the opinion of the one man who has understanding? Ought we not to fear and reverence him more than all the rest of the world: and if we desert him shall we not destroy and injure that principle in us which may be assumed to be improved by justice and deteriorated by injustice—there is such a principle?

CRITO: Certainly there is, Socrates.

SOCRATES: Take a parallel instance: if, acting under the advice of those who have no understanding, we destroy that which is improved by health and is deteriorated by disease, would life be worth having? And that which has been destroyed is—the body?

CRITO: Yes.

SOCRATES: Could we live, having an evil and corrupted body?

CRITO: Certainly not.

SOCRATES: And will life be worth having, if that higher part of man be destroyed, which is improved by justice and depraved by injustice? Do we suppose that principle, whatever it may be in man, which has to do with justice and injustice, to be inferior to the body?

CRITO: Certainly not.

SOCRATES: More honorable than the body?

CRITO: Far more.

SOCRATES: Then, my friend, we must not regard what the many say of us: but what he, the one man who has understanding of just and unjust, will say, and what the truth will say. And therefore you begin in error when you advise that we should regard the opinion of the many about just and unjust, good and evil, honorable and dishonorable.—'Well,' someone will say, 'but the many can kill us.'

CRITO: Yes, Socrates; that will clearly be the answer.

SOCRATES: And it is true; but still I find with surprise that the old argument is unshaken as ever. And I should like to know whether I may say the same of another proposition—that not life, but a good life, is to be chiefly valued?

CRITO: Yes, that also remains unshaken.

SOCRATES: And a good life is equivalent to a just and honorable one—that holds also?

CRITO: Yes, it does.

SOCRATES: From these premises I proceed to argue the question whether I ought or ought not to try and escape without the consent of the Athenians: and if I am clearly right in escaping, then I will make the attempt; but if not, I will abstain. The other considerations which you mention, of money and loss of character and the duty of educating one's children, are, I fear, only the doctrines of the multitude, who would be as ready to restore people to life, if they were able, as they are to put them to death—and with as little reason. But now, since the argument has thus far prevailed, the only question which remains to be considered is, whether we shall do rightly either in escaping or in suffering others to aid in our escape and paying them in money and thanks, or whether in reality we shall not do rightly; and if the latter, then death or any other calamity which may ensue on my remaining here must not be allowed to enter into the calculation.

CRITO: I think that you are right, Socrates; how then shall we proceed?

SOCRATES: Let us consider the matter together, and do you either refute me if you can, and I will be convinced; or else cease, my dear friend, from repeating to me that I ought to escape against the wishes of the Athenians: for I highly value your attempts to persuade me to do so, but I may not be persuaded against my own better judgment. And now please to consider my first position, and try how you can best answer me.

CRITO: I will.

SOCRATES: Are we to say that we are never intentionally to do wrong, or that in one way we ought and in another way we ought not to do wrong, or is doing wrong always evil and dishonorable, as I was just now saying, and as has been already acknowledged by us? Are all our former admissions which were made within a few days to be thrown away? And have we, at our age, been earnestly discoursing with one another all our life long only to discover that we are no better than children? Or, in spite of the opinion of the many, and in spite of consequences whether better or worse, shall we insist on the truth of what was then said, that injustice is always an evil and dishonour to him who acts unjustly? Shall we say so or not?

CRITO: Yes.

SOCRATES: Then we must do no wrong?

CRITO: Certainly not.

SOCRATES: Nor when injured injure in return, as the many imagine; for we must injure no one at all?[†]

CRITO: Clearly not.

SOCRATES: Again, Crito, may we do evil?

CRITO: Surely not, Socrates.

SOCRATES: And what of doing evil in return for evil, which is the morality of the many—is that just or not?

CRITO: Not just.

SOCRATES: For doing evil to another is the same as injuring him?

CRITO: Very true.

SOCRATES: Then we ought not to retaliate or render evil for evil to any one, whatever evil we may have suffered from him. But I would have you consider, Crito, whether you really mean what you are saying. For this opinion has never been held, and never will be held, by any considerable number of persons; and those who are agreed and those who are

[†] E.g. compare Rep.

not agreed upon this point have no common ground, and can only despise one another when they see how widely they differ. Tell me, then, whether you agree with and assent to my first principle, that neither injury nor retaliation nor warding off evil by evil is ever right. And shall that be the premiss of our argument? Or do you decline and dissent from this? For so I have ever thought, and continue to think; but, if you are of another opinion, let me hear what you have to say. If, however, you remain of the same mind as formerly, I will proceed to the next step.

CRITO: You may proceed, for I have not changed my mind.

SOCRATES: Then I will go on to the next point, which may be put in the form of a question:—Ought a man to do what he admits to be right, or ought he to betray the right?

CRITO: He ought to do what he thinks right.

SOCRATES: But if this is true, what is the application? In leaving the prison against the will of the Athenians, do I wrong any? or rather do I not wrong those whom I ought least to wrong? Do I not desert the principles which were acknowledged by us to be just—what do you say?

CRITO: I cannot tell, Socrates, for I do not know.

SOCRATES: Then consider the matter in this way: Imagine that I am about to play truant (you may call the proceeding by any name which you like), and the laws and the government come and interrogate me: 'Tell us, Socrates,' they say; 'what are you about? Are you not going by an act of yours to overturn us—the laws, and the whole state, as far as in you lies? Do you imagine that a state can subsist and not be overthrown, in which the decisions of law have no power, but are set aside and trampled upon by individuals?' What will be our answer, Crito, to these and the like words? Anyone, and especially a rhetorician, will have a good deal to say on behalf of the law which requires a sentence to be carried out. He will argue that this law should not be set aside; and shall we reply, 'Yes; but the state has injured us and given an unjust sentence.' Suppose I say that?

CRITO: Very good, Socrates.

SOCRATES: 'And was that our agreement with you?' the law would answer; 'or were you to abide by the sentence of the state?' And if I were to express my astonishment at their words, the law would probably add: 'Answer, Socrates, instead of opening your eyes—you are in the habit of asking and answering questions. Tell us—What complaint have you to make against us which justifies you in attempting to destroy us and the state? In the first place did we not bring you into existence? Your father married your mother by our aid and begat you. Say whether you have any objection to urge against those of us who regulate marriage?' None, I should reply. 'Or against those of us who after birth regulate the nurture and education of children, in which you also were trained? Were not the laws, which have the charge of education, right in commanding your father to train you in music and gymnastic?' Right, I should reply. 'Well then, since you were brought into the world and nurtured and educated by us, can you deny in the first place that you are our child and slave, as your fathers were before you? And if this is true you are not on equal terms with us; nor can you think that you have a right to do to us what we are doing to you. Would you have any right to strike or revile or do any other evil to your father or your master, if you had one, because you have been struck or reviled by him, or received some other evil at his hands? You would not say this? And because we think right to destroy you, do you think that you have any right to destroy us in return, and your country as far as in you lies? Will you, O professor of true virtue, pretend that you are justified in this? Has a philosopher like you failed to discover that our country is more to be valued and higher and holier far than mother or father or any ancestor, and more to be regarded in the eyes of the gods and of men of understanding? Also to be soothed, and gently and reverently entreated when angry, even more than a father, and either to be persuaded, or if not persuaded, to be obeyed? And when we are punished by her, whether with imprisonment or stripes, the punishment is to be endured in silence; and if she lead us to wounds or death in battle, thither we follow as is right; neither may anyone yield or retreat or leave his rank, but whether in battle or in a court of law, or in any other place, he must do what his city and his country order him; or he must change their view of what is just: and if he may do no violence to his father or mother, much less may he do violence to his country.' What answer shall we make to this, Crito? Do the laws speak truly, or do they not?

CRITO: I think that they do.

SOCRATES: Then the laws will say: 'Consider, Socrates, if we are speaking truly that in your present attempt you are going to do us an injury. For, having brought you into the world, and nurtured and educated you, and given you and every other citizen a share in every good which we had to give, we further proclaim to any Athenian by the liberty which we allow him, that if he does not like us when he has become of age and has seen the ways of the city, and made our acquaintance, he may go where he pleases and take his goods with him. None of us laws will forbid him or interfere with him. Anyone who does not like us and the city, and who wants to emigrate to a colony or to any other city, may go where he likes, retaining his property. But he who has experience of the manner in which we order justice and administer the state, and still remains, has entered into an implied contract that he will do as we command him. And he who disobeys us is, as we maintain, thrice wrong: first, because in disobeying us he is disobeying his parents; secondly, because we are the authors of his education; thirdly, because he has made an agreement with us that he will duly obey our commands; and he neither obeys them nor convinces us that our commands are unjust; and we do not rudely impose them, but give him the alternative of obeying or convincing us; that is what we offer, and he does neither. These are the sort of accusations to which, as we were saying, you, Socrates, will be exposed if you accomplish your intentions; you, above all other Athenians.' Suppose now I ask, why I rather than anybody else? They will justly retort upon me that I above all other men have acknowledged the agreement. 'There is clear proof,' they will say, 'Socrates, that we and the city were not displeasing to you. Of all Athenians you have been the most constant resident in the city, which, as you never leave, you may be supposed to love[†]. For you never went out of the city either to see the games, except once when you went to the Isthmus, or to any other place unless when you were on military service; nor did you travel as other men do. Nor had you any curiosity to know other states or their laws: your affections did not go beyond us and our state; we were your especial favourites, and you acquiesced in our government of you; and here in this city you begat your children, which is a proof of your satisfaction. Moreover, you might in the course of the trial, if you had liked, have fixed the penalty at banishment; the state which refuses to let you go now would have let you go then. But you pretended that you preferred death to exile[‡], and that you were not unwilling to die. And now you have forgotten these fine sentiments, and pay no respect to us the laws, of whom you are the destroyer; and are doing what only a miserable slave would do, running away and turning your back upon the compacts and agreements which you made as a citizen. And first of all answer this very question: Are we right in saying that you agreed to be governed according to us in deed, and not in word only? Is that true or not?' How shall we answer, Crito? Must we not assent?

CRITO: We cannot help it, Socrates.

SOCRATES: Then will they not say: 'You, Socrates, are breaking the covenants and agreements which you made

---

[†]compare Phaedr.
[‡]compare Apol.

with us at your leisure, not in any haste or under any compulsion or deception, but after you have had seventy years to think of them, during which time you were at liberty to leave the city, if we were not to your mind, or if our covenants appeared to you to be unfair. You had your choice, and might have gone either to Lacedaemon or Crete, both which states are often praised by you for their good government, or to some other Hellenic or foreign state. Whereas you, above all other Athenians, seemed to be so fond of the state, or, in other words, of us her laws (and who would care about a state which has no laws?), that you never stirred out of her; the halt, the blind, the maimed, were not more stationary in her than you were. And now you run away and forsake your agreements. Not so, Socrates, if you will take our advice; do not make yourself ridiculous by escaping out of the city. For just consider, if you transgress and err in this sort of way, what good will you do either to yourself or to your friends? That your friends will be driven into exile and deprived of citizenship, or will lose their property, is tolerably certain; and you yourself, if you fly to one of the neighbouring cities, as, for example, Thebes or Megara, both of which are well governed, will come to them as an enemy, Socrates, and their government will be against you, and all patriotic citizens will cast an evil eye upon you as a subverter of the laws, and you will confirm in the minds of the judges the justice of their own condemnation of you. For he who is a corrupter of the laws is more than likely to be a corrupter of the young and foolish portion of mankind. Will you then flee from well-ordered cities and virtuous men? And is existence worth having on these terms? Or will you go to them without shame, and talk to them, Socrates? And what will you say to them? What you say here about virtue and justice and institutions and laws being the best things among men? Would that be decent of you? Surely not. But if you go away from well-governed states to Crito's friends in Thessaly, where there is great disorder and licence, they will be charmed to hear the tale of your escape from prison, set off with ludicrous particulars of the manner in which you were wrapped in a goatskin or some other disguise, and metamorphosed as the manner is of runaways; but will there be no one to remind you that in your old age you were not ashamed to violate the most sacred laws from a miserable desire of a little more life? Perhaps not, if you keep them in a good temper; but if they are out of temper you will hear many degrading things; you will live, but how?—as the flatterer of all men, and the servant of all men; and doing what?—eating and drinking in Thessaly, having gone abroad in order that you may get a dinner. And where will be your fine sentiments about justice and virtue? Say that you wish to live for the sake of your children—you want to bring them up and educate them—will you take them into Thessaly and deprive them of Athenian citizenship? Is this the benefit which you will confer upon them? Or are you under the impression that they will be better cared for and educated here if you are still alive, although absent from them; for your friends will take care of them? Do you fancy that if you are an inhabitant of Thessaly they will take care of them, and if you are an inhabitant of the other world that they will not take care of them? Nay; but if they who call themselves friends are good for anything, they will—to be sure they will. Listen, then, Socrates, to us who have brought you up. Think not of life and children first, and of justice afterwards, but of justice first, that you may be justified before the princes of the world below. For neither will you nor any that belong to you be happier or holier or juster in this life, or happier in another, if you do as Crito bids. Now you depart in innocence, a sufferer and not a doer of evil; a victim, not of the laws, but of men. But if you go forth, returning evil for evil, and injury for injury, breaking the covenants and agreements which you have made with us, and wronging those whom you ought least of all to wrong, that is to say, yourself, your friends, your country, and us, we shall be angry with you while you live, and our brethren, the laws in the world below, will receive you as an enemy; for they will know that you have done your best to destroy us. Listen, then, to us and not to Crito.' This, dear Crito, is the voice which I seem to hear murmuring in my ears, like the sound of the flute in the ears of the mystic; that voice, I say, is humming in my ears, and prevents me from hearing any other. And I know that anything more which you may say will be vain. Yet speak, if you have anything to say.

CRITO: I have nothing to say, Socrates.

SOCRATES: Leave me then, Crito, to fulfilll the will of God, and to follow whither he leads.

LYSIS

PERSONS OF THE DIALOGUE: Socrates, who is the narrator, Menexenus, Hippothales, Lysis, Ctesippus.
SCENE: A newly-erected Palaestra outside the walls of Athens.

I was going from the Academy straight to the Lyceum, intending to take the outer road, which is close under the wall. When I came to the postern gate of the city, which is by the fountain of Panops, I fell in with Hippothales, the son of Hieronymus, and Ctesippus the Paeanian, and a company of young men who were standing with them. Hippothales, seeing me approach, asked whence I came and whither I was going.

'I am going,' I replied, 'from the Academy straight to the Lyceum.'

'Then come straight to us,' he said, 'and put in here; you may as well.'

'Who are you,' I said; 'and where am I to come?'

He showed me an enclosed space and an open door over against the wall. 'And there,' he said, 'is the building at which we all meet: and a goodly company we are.'

'And what is this building,' I asked; 'and what sort of entertainment have you?'

'The building,' he replied, 'is a newly erected Palaestra; and the entertainment is generally conversation, to which you are welcome.'

'Thank you,' I said; 'and is there any teacher there?'

'Yes,' he said, 'your old friend and admirer, Miccus.'

'Indeed,' I replied; 'he is a very eminent professor.'

'Are you disposed,' he said, 'to go with me and see them?'

'Yes,' I said; 'but I should like to know first, what is expected of me, and who is the favourite among you?'

'Some persons have one favorite, Socrates, and some another,' he said.

'And who is yours?' I asked: 'tell me that, Hippothales.'

At this he blushed; and I said to him, 'O Hippothales, thou son of Hieronymus! Do not say that you are, or that you are not, in love; the confession is too late; for I see that you are not only in love, but are already far gone in your love. Simple and foolish as I am, the gods have given me the power of understanding affections of this kind.'

Whereupon he blushed more and more.

Ctesippus said: 'I like to see you blushing, Hippothales, and hesitating to tell Socrates the name; when, if he were with you but for a very short time, you would have plagued him to death by talking about nothing else. Indeed, Socrates, he has literally deafened us, and stopped our ears with the praises of Lysis; and if he is a little intoxicated, there is every likelihood that we may have our sleep murdered with a cry of Lysis. His performances in prose are bad enough, but nothing at all in comparison with his verse; and when he drenches us with his poems and other compositions, it is really too bad; and worse still is his manner of singing them to his love; he has a voice which is truly appalling, and we cannot help hearing him: and now having a question put to him by you, behold he is blushing.'

'Who is Lysis?' I said: 'I suppose that he must be young; for the name does not recall anyone to me.'

'Why,' he said, 'his father being a very well-known man, he retains his patronymic, and is not as yet commonly called by his own name; but, although you do not know his name, I am sure that you must know his face, for that is quite enough to distinguish him.'

'But tell me whose son he is,' I said.

'He is the eldest son of Democrates, of the deme of Aexone.'

'Ah, Hippothales,' I said; 'what a noble and really perfect love you have found! I wish that you would favour me with the exhibition which you have been making to the rest of the company, and then I shall be able to judge whether you know what a lover ought to say about his love, either to the youth himself, or to others.'

'Nay, Socrates,' he said; 'you surely do not attach any importance to what he is saying.'

'Do you mean,' I said, 'that you disown the love of the person whom he says that you love?'

'No; but I deny that I make verses or address compositions to him.'

'He is not in his right mind,' said Ctesippus; 'he is talking nonsense, and is stark mad.'

'O Hippothales,' I said, 'if you have ever made any verses or songs in honor of your favorite, I do not want to hear them; but I want to know the purport of them, that I may be able to judge of your mode of approaching your fair one.'

'Ctesippus will be able to tell you,' he said; 'for if, as he avers, the sound of my words is always dinning in his ears, he must have a very accurate knowledge and recollection of them.'

'Yes, indeed,' said Ctesippus; 'I know only too well; and very ridiculous the tale is: for although he is a lover, and very devotedly in love, he has nothing particular to talk about to his beloved which a child might not say. Now is not that ridiculous? He can only speak of the wealth of Democrates, which the whole city celebrates, and grandfather Lysis, and the other ancestors of the youth, and their stud of horses, and their victory at the Pythian games, and at the Isthmus, and at Nemea with four horses and single horses—these are the tales which he composes and repeats. And there is greater twaddle still. Only the day before yesterday he made a poem in which he described the entertainment of Heracles, who was a connexion of the family, setting forth how in virtue of this relationship he was hospitably received by an ancestor of Lysis; this ancestor was himself begotten of Zeus by the daughter of the founder of the deme. And these are the sort of old wives' tales which he sings and recites to us, and we are obliged to listen to him.'

When I heard this, I said: 'O ridiculous Hippothales! How can you be making and singing hymns in honor of yourself before you have won?'

'But my songs and verses,' he said, 'are not in honour of myself, Socrates.'

'You think not?' I said.

'Nay, but what do you think?' he replied.

'Most assuredly,' I said, 'those songs are all in your own honor; for if you win your beautiful love, your discourses and songs will be a glory to you, and may be truly regarded as hymns of praise composed in honor of you who have conquered and won such a love; but if he slips away from you, the more you have praised him, the more ridiculous you will look at having lost this fairest and best of blessings; and therefore the wise lover does not praise his beloved until he has won him, because he is afraid of accidents. There is also another danger; the fair, when anyone praises or magnifies them, are filled with the spirit of pride and vain-glory. Do you not agree with me?'

'Yes,' he said.

'And the more vain-glorious they are, the more difficult is the capture of them?'

'I believe you.'

'What should you say of a hunter who frightened away his prey, and made the capture of the animals which he is hunting more difficult?'

'He would be a bad hunter, undoubtedly.'

'Yes; and if, instead of soothing them, he were to infuriate them with words and songs, that would show a great want of wit: do you not agree.'

'Yes.'

'And now reflect, Hippothales, and see whether you are not guilty of all these errors in writing poetry. For I can hardly suppose that you will affirm a man to be a good poet who injures himself by his poetry.'

'Assuredly not,' he said; 'such a poet would be a fool. And this is the reason why I take you into my counsels, Socrates, and I shall be glad of any further advice which you may have to offer. Will you tell me by what words or actions I may become endeared to my love?'

'That is not easy to determine,' I said; 'but if you will bring your love to me, and will let me talk with him, I may perhaps be able to show you how to converse with him, instead of singing and reciting in the fashion of which you are accused.'

'There will be no difficulty in bringing him,' he replied; 'if you will only go with Ctesippus into the Palaestra, and sit down and talk, I believe that he will come of his own accord; for he is fond of listening, Socrates. And as this is the festival of the Hermaea, the young men and boys are all together, and there is no separation between them. He will be sure to come: but if he does not, Ctesippus with whom he is familiar, and whose relation Menexenus is his great friend, shall call him.'

'That will be the way,' I said. 'Thereupon I led Ctesippus into the Palaestra, and the rest followed.'

Upon entering we found that the boys had just been sacrificing; and this part of the festival was nearly at an end. They were all in their white array, and games at dice were going on among them. Most of them were in the outer court amusing themselves; but some were in a corner of the Apodyterium playing at odd and even with a number of dice, which they took out of little wicker baskets. There was also a circle of lookers-on; among them was Lysis. He was standing with the other boys and youths, having a crown upon his head, like a fair vision, and not less worthy of praise for his goodness than for his beauty. We left them, and went over to the opposite side of the room, where, finding a quiet place, we sat down; and then we began to talk. This attracted Lysis, who was constantly turning round to look at us—he was evidently wanting to come to us. For a time he hesitated and had not the courage to come alone; but first of all, his friend Menexenus, leaving his play, entered the Palaestra from the court, and when he saw Ctesippus and myself, was going to take a seat by us; and then Lysis, seeing him, followed, and sat down by his side; and the other boys joined. I should observe that Hippothales, when he saw the crowd, got behind them, where he thought that he would be out of sight of Lysis, lest he should anger him; and there he stood and listened.

I turned to Menexenus, and said: 'Son of Demophon, which of you two youths is the elder?'

'That is a matter of dispute between us,' he said.

'And which is the nobler? Is that also a matter of dispute?'

'Yes, certainly.'

'And another disputed point is, which is the fairer?'

The two boys laughed.

'I shall not ask which is the richer of the two,' I said; 'for you are friends, are you not?'

'Certainly,' they replied.

'And friends have all things in common, so that one of you can be no richer than the other, if you say truly that you are friends.'

They assented. I was about to ask which was the juster of the two, and which was the wiser of the two; but at this moment Menexenus was called away by someone who came and said that the gymnastic-master wanted him. I supposed that he had to offer sacrifice. So he went away, and I asked Lysis some more questions. 'I dare say, Lysis,' I said, 'that your father and mother love you very much.'

'Certainly,' he said.

'And they would wish you to be perfectly happy.'

'Yes.'

'But do you think that anyone is happy who is in the condition of a slave, and who cannot do what he likes?'

'I should think not indeed,' he said.

'And if your father and mother love you, and desire that you should be happy, no one can doubt that they are very ready to promote your happiness.'

'Certainly,' he replied.

'And do they then permit you to do what you like, and never rebuke you or hinder you from doing what you desire?'

'Yes, indeed, Socrates; there are a great many things which they hinder me from doing.'

'What do you mean?' I said. 'Do they want you to be happy, and yet hinder you from doing what you like? For example, if you want to mount one of your father's chariots, and take the reins at a race, they will not allow you to do so—they will prevent you?'

'Certainly,' he said, 'they will not allow me to do so.'

'Whom then will they allow?'

'There is a charioteer, whom my father pays for driving.'

'And do they trust a hireling more than you? And may he do what he likes with the horses? And do they pay him for this?'

'They do.'

'But I dare say that you may take the whip and guide the mule-cart if you like—they will permit that?'

'Permit me! Indeed they will not.'

'Then,' I said, 'may no one use the whip to the mules?'

'Yes,' he said, 'the muleteer.'

'And is he a slave or a free man?' 'A slave,' he said.

'And do they esteem a slave of more value than you who are their son? And do they entrust their property to him rather than to you? And allow him to do what he likes, when they prohibit you? Answer me now: Are you your own master, or do they not even allow that?'

'Nay,' he said; 'of course they do not allow it.'

'Then you have a master?'

'Yes, my tutor; there he is.'

'And is he a slave?'

'To be sure; he is our slave,' he replied.

'Surely,' I said, 'this is a strange thing, that a free man should be governed by a slave. And what does he do with you?'

'He takes me to my teachers.'

'You do not mean to say that your teachers also rule over you?'

'Of course they do.'

'Then I must say that your father is pleased to inflict many lords and masters on you. But at any rate when you go home to your mother, she will let you have your own way, and will not interfere with your happiness; her wool, or the piece of cloth which she is weaving, are at your disposal: I am sure that there is nothing to hinder you from touching her wooden spathe, or her comb, or any other of her spinning implements.'

'Nay, Socrates,' he replied, laughing; 'not only does she hinder me, but I should be beaten if I were to touch one of them.'

'Well,' I said, 'this is amazing. And did you ever behave ill to your father or your mother?'

'No, indeed,' he replied.

'But why then are they so terribly anxious to prevent you from being happy, and doing as you like?—keeping you all day long in subjection to another, and, in a word, doing nothing which you desire; so that you have no good, as would appear, out of their great possessions, which are under the control of anybody rather than of you, and have no use of your own fair person, which is tended and taken care of by another; while you, Lysis, are master of nobody, and can do nothing?'

'Why,' he said, 'Socrates, the reason is that I am not of age.'

'I doubt whether that is the real reason,' I said; 'for I should imagine that your father Democrates, and your mother, do permit you to do many things already, and do not wait until you are of age: for example, if they want anything read or written, you, I presume, would be the first person in the house who is summoned by them.'

'Very true.'

'And you would be allowed to write or read the letters in any order which you please, or to take up the lyre and tune the notes, and play with the fingers, or strike with the plectrum, exactly as you please, and neither father nor mother would interfere with you.'

'That is true,' he said.

'Then what can be the reason, Lysis,' I said, 'why they allow you to do the one and not the other?'

'I suppose,' he said, 'because I understand the one, and not the other.'

'Yes, my dear youth,' I said, 'the reason is not any deficiency of years, but a deficiency of knowledge; and whenever your father thinks that you are wiser than he is, he will instantly commit himself and his possessions to you.'

'I think so.'

'Aye,' I said; 'and about your neighbour, too, does not the same rule hold as about your father? If he is satisfied that you know more of housekeeping than he does, will he continue to administer his affairs himself, or will he commit them to you?'

'I think that he will commit them to me.'

'Will not the Athenian people, too, entrust their affairs to you when they see that you have wisdom enough to manage them?'

'Yes.'

'And oh! Let me put another case,' I said: 'There is the great king, and he has an eldest son, who is the Prince of Asia—suppose that you and I go to him and establish to his satisfaction that we are better cooks than his son, will he not entrust to us the prerogative of making soup, and putting in anything that we like while the pot is boiling, rather than to the Prince of Asia, who is his son?'

'To us, clearly.'

'And we shall be allowed to throw in salt by handfuls, whereas the son will not be allowed to put in as much as he can take up between his fingers?'

'Of course.'

'Or suppose again that the son has bad eyes, will he allow him, or will he not allow him, to touch his own eyes if he thinks that he has no knowledge of medicine?'

'He will not allow him.'

'Whereas, if he supposes us to have a knowledge of medicine, he will allow us to do what we like with him—even to open the eyes wide and sprinkle ashes upon them, because he supposes that we know what is best?'

'That is true.'

'And everything in which we appear to him to be wiser than himself or his son he will commit to us?'

'That is very true, Socrates,' he replied.

'Then now, my dear Lysis,' I said, 'you perceive that in things which we know everyone will trust us—Hellenes and barbarians, men and women—and we may do as we please about them, and no one will like to interfere with us; we shall be free, and masters of others; and these things will be really ours, for we shall be benefited by them. But in things of which we have no understanding, no one will trust us to do as seems good to us—they will hinder us as far as they can; and not only strangers, but father and mother, and the friend, if there be one, who is dearer still, will also hinder us; and we shall be subject to others; and these things will not be ours, for we shall not be benefited by them. Do you agree?'

He assented.

'And shall we be friends to others, and will any others love us, in as far as we are useless to them?'

'Certainly not.'

'Neither can your father or mother love you, nor can anybody love anybody else, in so far as they are useless to them?'

'No.'

'And therefore, my boy, if you are wise, all men will be your friends and kindred, for you will be useful and good; but if you are not wise, neither father, nor mother, nor kindred, nor anyone else, will be your friends.'

'And in matters of which you have as yet no knowledge, can you have any conceit of knowledge?'

'That is impossible,' he replied.

'And you, Lysis, if you require a teacher, have not yet attained to wisdom.'

'True.'

'And therefore you are not conceited, having nothing of which to be conceited.'

'Indeed, Socrates, I think not.'

When I heard him say this, I turned to Hippothales, and was very nearly making a blunder, for I was going to say to him: 'That is the way, Hippothales, in which you should talk to your beloved, humbling and lowering him, and not as you do, puffing him up and spoiling him.' But I saw that he was in great excitement and confusion at what had been said, and I remembered that, although he was in the neighbourhood, he did not want to be seen by Lysis; so upon second thoughts I refrained.

In the meantime Menexenus came back and sat down in his place by Lysis; and Lysis, in a childish and affectionate manner, whispered privately in my ear, so that Menexenus should not hear: 'Do, Socrates, tell Menexenus what you have been telling me.'

'Suppose that you tell him yourself, Lysis,' I replied; 'for I am sure that you were attending.'

'Certainly,' he replied.

'Try, then, to remember the words, and be as exact as you can in repeating them to him, and if you have forgotten anything, ask me again the next time that you see me.'

'I will be sure to do so, Socrates; but go on telling him something new, and let me hear, as long as I am allowed to stay.'

'I certainly cannot refuse,' I said, 'since you ask me; but then, as you know, Menexenus is very pugnacious, and therefore you must come to the rescue if he attempts to upset me.'

'Yes, indeed,' he said; 'he is very pugnacious, and that is the reason why I want you to argue with him.'

'That I may make a fool of myself?'

'No, indeed,' he said; 'but I want you to put him down.'

'That is no easy matter, I replied; for he is a terrible fellow—a pupil of Ctesippus. And there is Ctesippus himself: do you see him?'

'Never mind, Socrates, you shall argue with him.'

'Well, I suppose that I must,' I replied.

Hereupon Ctesippus complained that we were talking in secret, and keeping the feast to ourselves.

'I shall be happy,' I said, 'to let you have a share. Here is Lysis, who does not understand something that I was saying, and wants me to ask Menexenus, who, as he thinks, is likely to know.'

'And why do you not ask him?' he said.

'Very well,' I said, 'I will; and do you, Menexenus, answer. But first I must tell you that I am one who from my childhood upward have set my heart upon a certain thing. All people have their fancies; some desire horses, and others dogs; and some are fond of gold, and others of honor. Now, I have no violent desire of any of these things; but I have a passion for friends; and I would rather have a good friend than the best cock or quail in the world: I would even go further, and say the best horse or dog. Yea, by the dog of Egypt, I should greatly prefer a real friend to all the gold of Darius, or even to Darius himself: I am such a lover of friends as that. And when I see you and Lysis, at your early age, so easily possessed of this treasure, and so soon, he of you, and you of him, I am amazed and delighted, seeing that I myself, although I am now advanced in years, am so far from having made a similar acquisition, that I do not even know in what way a friend is acquired. But I want to ask you a question about this, for you have experience: tell me then, when one loves another, is the lover or the beloved the friend; or may either be the friend?'

'Either may, I should think, be the friend of either.'

'Do you mean,' I said, 'that if only one of them loves the other, they are mutual friends?'

'Yes,' he said; 'that is my meaning.'

'But what if the lover is not loved in return? Which is a very possible case.'

'Yes.'

'Or is, perhaps, even hated? Which is a fancy which sometimes is entertained by lovers respecting their beloved. Nothing can exceed their love; and yet they imagine either that they are not loved in return, or that they are hated. Is not that true?'

'Yes,' he said, 'quite true.'

'In that case, the one loves, and the other is loved?'

'Yes.'

'Then which is the friend of which? Is the lover the friend of the beloved, whether he be loved in return, or hated; or is the beloved the friend; or is there no friendship at all on either side, unless they both love one another?'

'There would seem to be none at all.'

'Then this notion is not in accordance with our previous one. We were saying that both were friends, if one only loved; but now, unless they both love, neither is a friend.'

'That appears to be true.'

'Then nothing which does not love in return is beloved by a lover?'

'I think not.'

'Then they are not lovers of horses, whom the horses do not love in return; nor lovers of quails, nor of dogs, nor of wine, nor of gymnastic exercises, who have no return of love; no, nor of wisdom, unless wisdom loves them in return. Or shall we say that they do love them, although they are not beloved by them; and that the poet was wrong who sings—"Happy the man to whom his children are dear, and steeds having single hoofs, and dogs of chase, and the stranger of another land"?

'I do not think that he was wrong.'

'You think that he is right?'

'Yes.'

'Then, Menexenus, the conclusion is, that what is beloved, whether loving or hating, may be dear to the lover of it: for example, very young children, too young to love, or even hating their father or mother when they are punished by them, are never dearer to them than at the time when they are being hated by them.'

'I think that what you say is true.'

'And, if so, not the lover, but the beloved, is the friend or dear one?'

'Yes.'

'And the hated one, and not the hater, is the enemy?'

'Clearly.'

'Then many men are loved by their enemies, and hated by their friends, and are the friends of their enemies, and the enemies of their friends. Yet how absurd, my dear friend, or indeed impossible is this paradox of a man being an enemy to his friend or a friend to his enemy.'

'I quite agree, Socrates, in what you say.'

'But if this cannot be, the lover will be the friend of that which is loved?'

'True.'

'And the hater will be the enemy of that which is hated?'

'Certainly.'

'Yet we must acknowledge in this, as in the preceding instance, that a man may be the friend of one who is not his friend, or who may be his enemy, when he loves that which does not love him or which even hates him. And he may be the enemy of one who is not his enemy, and is even his friend: for example, when he hates that which does not hate him, or which even loves him.'

'That appears to be true.'

'But if the lover is not a friend, nor the beloved a friend, nor both together, what are we to say? Whom are we to call friends to one another? Do any remain?'

'Indeed, Socrates, I cannot find any.'

'But, O Menexenus! I said, may we not have been altogether wrong in our conclusions?'

'I am sure that we have been wrong, Socrates,' said Lysis. 'And he blushed as he spoke, the words seeming to come from his lips involuntarily, because his whole mind was taken up with the argument; there was no mistaking his attentive look while he was listening.

I was pleased at the interest which was shown by Lysis, and I wanted to give Menexenus a rest, so I turned to him and said, 'I think, Lysis, that what you say is true, and that, if we had been right, we should never have gone so far wrong; let us proceed no further in this direction (for the road seems to be getting troublesome), but take the other path into which we turned, and see what the poets have to say; for they are to us in a manner the fathers and authors of wisdom, and they speak of friends in no light or trivial manner, but God himself, as they say, makes them and draws them to one another; and this they express, if I am not mistaken, in the following words: "God is ever drawing like towards like, and making them acquainted." I dare say that you have heard those words.'

'Yes,' he said; 'I have.'

'And have you not also met with the treatises of philosophers who say that like must love like? They are the people who argue and write about nature and the universe.'

'Very true,' he replied.

'And are they right in saying this?'

'They may be.'

'Perhaps,' I said, 'about half, or possibly, altogether, right, if their meaning were rightly apprehended by us. For the more a bad man has to do with a bad man, and the more nearly he is brought into contact with him, the more he will be likely to hate him, for he injures him; and injurer and injured cannot be friends. Is not that true?'

'Yes,' he said.

'Then one half of the saying is untrue, if the wicked are like one another?'

'That is true.'

'But the real meaning of the saying, as I imagine, is, that the good are like one another, and friends to one another; and that the bad, as is often said of them, are never at unity with one another or with themselves; for they are passionate and restless, and anything which is at variance and enmity with itself is not likely to be in union or harmony with any other thing. Do you not agree?'

'Yes, I do.'

'Then, my friend, those who say that the like is friendly to the like mean to intimate, if I rightly apprehend them, that the good only is the friend of the good, and of him only; but that the evil never attains to any real friendship, either with good or evil. Do you agree?'

He nodded assent.

'Then now we know how to answer the question "Who are friends?" for the argument declares "That the good are friends."'

'Yes,' he said, 'that is true.'

'Yes,' I replied; 'and yet I am not quite satisfied with this answer. By heaven, and shall I tell you what I suspect? I will. Assuming that like, inasmuch as he is like, is the friend of like, and useful to him—or rather let me try another way of putting the matter: Can like do any good or harm to like which he could not do to himself, or suffer anything from his like which he would not suffer from himself? And if neither can be of any use to the other, how can they be loved by one another? Can they now?'

'They cannot.'

'And can he who is not loved be a friend?'

'Certainly not.'

'But say that the like is not the friend of the like in so far as he is like; still the good may be the friend of the good in so far as he is good?'

'True.'

'But then again, will not the good, in so far as he is good, be sufficient for himself? Certainly he will. And he who is sufficient wants nothing—that is implied in the word sufficient.'

'Of course not.'

'And he who wants nothing will desire nothing?'

'He will not.'

'Neither can he love that which he does not desire?'

'He cannot.'

'And he who loves not is not a lover or friend?'

'Clearly not.'

'What place then is there for friendship, if, when absent, good men have no need of one another (for even when alone they are sufficient for themselves), and when present have no use of one another? How can such persons ever be induced to value one another?'

'They cannot.'

'And friends they cannot be, unless they value one another?'

'Very true.'

'But see now, Lysis, whether we are not being deceived in all this—are we not indeed entirely wrong?'

'How so?' he replied.

'Have I not heard someone say, as I just now recollect, that the like is the greatest enemy of the like, the good of the good?—Yes, and he quoted the authority of Hesiod, who says: "Potter quarrels with potter, bard with bard, beggar with beggar"; and of all other things he affirmed, in like manner, "That of necessity the most like are most full of envy, strife, and hatred of one another, and the most unlike, of friendship. For the poor man is compelled to be the friend of the rich, and the weak requires the aid of the strong, and the sick man of the physician; and everyone who is ignorant, has to love and court him who knows." And indeed he went on to say in grandiloquent language, that the idea of friendship existing between similars is not the truth, but the very reverse of the truth, and that the most opposed are the most friendly; for that everything desires not like but that which is most unlike: for example, the dry desires the moist, the cold the hot, the bitter the sweet, the sharp the blunt, the void the full, the full the void, and so of all other things; for the opposite is the food of the opposite, whereas like receives nothing from like. And I thought that he who said this was a charming man, and that he spoke well. What do the rest of you say?'

'I should say, at first hearing, that he is right,' said Menexenus.

'Then we are to say that the greatest friendship is of opposites?'

'Exactly.'

'Yes, Menexenus; but will not that be a monstrous answer? and will not the all-wise eristics be down upon us in triumph, and ask, fairly enough, whether love is not the very opposite of hate; and what answer shall we make to them—must we not admit that they speak the truth?'

'We must.'

'They will then proceed to ask whether the enemy is the friend of the friend, or the friend the friend of the enemy?'

'Neither,' he replied.

'Well, but is a just man the friend of the unjust, or the temperate of the intemperate, or the good of the bad?'

'I do not see how that is possible.'

'And yet,' I said, 'if friendship goes by contraries, the contraries must be friends.'

'They must.'

'Then neither like and like nor unlike and unlike are friends.'

'I suppose not.'

'And yet there is a further consideration: may not all these notions of friendship be erroneous? But may not that which is neither good nor evil still in some cases be the friend of the good?'

'How do you mean?' he said.

'Why really,' I said, 'the truth is that I do not know; but my head is dizzy with thinking of the argument, and therefore I hazard the conjecture, that "the beautiful is the friend," as the old proverb says. Beauty is certainly a soft, smooth, slippery thing, and therefore of a nature which easily slips in and permeates our souls. For I affirm that the good is the beautiful. You will agree to that?'

'Yes.'

'This I say from a sort of notion that what is neither good nor evil is the friend of the beautiful and the good, and I will tell you why I am inclined to think so: I assume that there are three principles—the good, the bad, and that which is neither good nor bad. You would agree—would you not?'

'I agree.'

'And neither is the good the friend of the good, nor the evil of the evil, nor the good of the evil; these alternatives are excluded by the previous argument; and therefore, if there be such a thing as friendship or love at all, we must infer that what is neither good nor evil must be the friend, either of the good, or of that which is neither good nor evil, for nothing can be the friend of the bad.'

'True.'

'But neither can like be the friend of like, as we were just now saying.'

'True.'

'And if so, that which is neither good nor evil can have no friend which is neither good nor evil.'

'Clearly not.'

'Then the good alone is the friend of that only which is neither good nor evil.'

'That may be assumed to be certain.'

'And does not this seem to put us in the right way? Just remark, that the body which is in health requires neither medical nor any other aid, but is well enough; and the healthy man has no love of the physician, because he is in health.'

'He has none.'

'But the sick loves him, because he is sick?'

'Certainly.'

'And sickness is an evil, and the art of medicine a good and useful thing?'

'Yes.'

'But the human body, regarded as a body, is neither good nor evil?'

'True.'

'And the body is compelled by reason of disease to court and make friends of the art of medicine?'

'Yes.'

'Then that which is neither good nor evil becomes the friend of good, by reason of the presence of evil?'

'So we may infer.'

'And clearly this must have happened before that which was neither good nor evil had become altogether corrupted with the element of evil—if itself had become evil it would not still desire and love the good; for, as we were saying, the evil cannot be the friend of the good.'

'Impossible.'

'Further, I must observe that some substances are assimilated when others are present with them; and there are some which are not assimilated: take, for example, the case of an ointment or color which is put on another substance.'

'Very good.'

'In such a case, is the substance which is anointed the same as the colour or ointment?'

'What do you mean?' he said.

'This is what I mean: Suppose that I were to cover your auburn locks with white lead, would they be really white, or would they only appear to be white?'

'They would only appear to be white,' he replied.

'And yet whiteness would be present in them?'

'True.'

'But that would not make them at all the more white, notwithstanding the presence of white in them—they would not be white any more than black?'

'No.'

'But when old age infuses whiteness into them, then they become assimilated, and are white by the presence of white.'

'Certainly.'

'Now I want to know whether in all cases a substance is assimilated by the presence of another substance; or must the presence be after a peculiar sort?'

'The latter,' he said.

'Then that which is neither good nor evil may be in the presence of evil, but not as yet evil, and that has happened before now?'

'Yes.'

'And when anything is in the presence of evil, not being as yet evil, the presence of good arouses the desire of good in that thing;

but the presence of evil, which makes a thing evil, takes away the desire and friendship of the good; for that which was once both good and evil has now become evil only, and the good was supposed to have no friendship with the evil?'

'None.'

'And therefore we say that those who are already wise, whether gods or men, are no longer lovers of wisdom; nor can they be lovers of wisdom who are ignorant to the extent of being evil, for no evil or ignorant person is a lover of wisdom. There remain those who have the misfortune to be ignorant, but are not yet hardened in their ignorance, or void of understanding, and do not as yet fancy that they know what they do not know: and therefore those who are the lovers of wisdom are as yet neither good nor bad. But the bad do not love wisdom any more than the good; for, as we have already seen, neither is unlike the friend of unlike, nor like of like. You remember that?'

'Yes,' they both said.

'And so, Lysis and Menexenus, we have discovered the nature of friendship—there can be no doubt of it: Friendship is the love which by reason of the presence of evil the neither good nor evil has of the good, either in the soul, or in the body, or anywhere.'

They both agreed and entirely assented, and for a moment I rejoiced and was satisfied like a huntsman just holding fast his prey. But then a most unaccountable suspicion came across me, and I felt that the conclusion was untrue. I was pained, and said, 'Alas! Lysis and Menexenus, I am afraid that we have been grasping at a shadow only.'

'Why do you say so?' said Menexenus.

'I am afraid,' I said, 'that the argument about friendship is false: arguments, like men, are often pretenders.'

'How do you mean?' he asked.

'Well,' I said; 'look at the matter in this way: a friend is the friend of someone; is he not?'

'Certainly he is.'

'And has he a motive and object in being a friend, or has he no motive and object?'

'He has a motive and object.'

'And is the object which makes him a friend, dear to him, or neither dear nor hateful to him?'

'I do not quite follow you,' he said.

'I do not wonder at that,' I said. 'But perhaps, if I put the matter in another way, you will be able to follow me, and my own meaning will be clearer to myself. The sick man, as I was just now saying, is the friend of the physician—is he not?'

'Yes.'

'And he is the friend of the physician because of disease, and for the sake of health?'

'Yes.'

'And disease is an evil?'

'Certainly.'

'And what of health?' I said. 'Is that good or evil, or neither?'

'Good,' he replied.

'And we were saying, I believe, that the body being neither good nor evil, because of disease, that is to say because of evil, is the friend of medicine, and medicine is a good: and medicine has entered into this friendship for the sake of health, and health is a good.'

'True.'

'And is health a friend, or not a friend?'

'A friend.'

'And disease is an enemy?'

'Yes.'

'Then that which is neither good nor evil is the friend of the good because of the evil and hateful, and for the sake of the good and the friend?'

'Clearly.'

'Then the friend is a friend for the sake of the friend, and because of the enemy?'

'That is to be inferred.'

'Then at this point, my boys, let us take heed, and be on our guard against deceptions. I will not again repeat that the friend is the friend of the friend, and the like of the like, which has been declared by us to be an impossibility; but, in order that this new statement may not delude us, let us attentively examine another point, which I will proceed to explain: Medicine, as we were saying, is a friend, or dear to us for the sake of health?'

'Yes.'

'And health is also dear?'

'Certainly.'

'And if dear, then dear for the sake of something?'

'Yes.'

'And surely this object must also be dear, as is implied in our previous admissions?'

'Yes.'

'And that something dear involves something else dear?'

'Yes.'

'But then, proceeding in this way, shall we not arrive at some first principle of friendship or dearness which is not capable of being referred to any other, for the sake of which, as we maintain, all other things are dear, and, having there arrived, we shall stop?'

'True.'

'My fear is that all those other things, which, as we say, are dear for the sake of another, are illusions and deceptions only, but where that first principle is, there is the true ideal of friendship. Let me put the matter thus: Suppose the case of a great treasure (this may be a son, who is more precious to his father than all his other treasures); would not the father, who values his son above all things, value other things also for the sake of his son? I mean, for instance, if he knew that his son had drunk hemlock, and the father thought that wine would save him, he would value the wine?'

'He would.'

'And also the vessel which contains the wine?'

'Certainly.'

'But does he therefore value the three measures of wine, or the earthen vessel which contains them, equally with his son? Is not this rather the true state of the case? All his anxiety has regard not to the means which are provided for the sake of an object, but to the object for the sake of which they are provided. And although we may often say that gold and silver are highly valued by us, that is not the truth; for there is a further object, whatever it may be, which we value most of all, and for the sake of which gold and all our other possessions are acquired by us. Am I not right?'

'Yes, certainly.'

'And may not the same be said of the friend? That which is only dear to us for the sake of something else is improperly said to be dear, but the truly dear is that in which all these so-called dear friendships terminate.'

'That,' he said, 'appears to be true.'

'And the truly dear or ultimate principle of friendship is not for the sake of any other or further dear.'

'True.'

'Then we have done with the notion that friendship has any further object. May we then infer that the good is the friend?'

'I think so.'

'And the good is loved for the sake of the evil? Let me put the case in this way: Suppose that of the three principles, good, evil, and that which is neither good nor evil, there remained only the good and the neutral, and that evil went far away, and in no way affected soul or body, nor ever at all that class of things which, as we say, are neither good nor evil in themselves—would the good be of any use, or other than useless to us? For if there were nothing to hurt us any longer, we should have no need of anything that would do us good. Then would be clearly seen that we did but love and desire the good because of the evil, and as the remedy of the evil, which was the disease; but if there had been no disease, there would have been no need of a remedy. Is not this the nature of the good—to be loved by us who are placed between the two, because of the evil? But there is no use in the good for its own sake.'

'I suppose not.'

'Then the final principle of friendship, in which all other friendships terminated, those, I mean, which are relatively dear and for the sake of something else, is of another and a different nature from them. For they are called dear because of another dear or friend. But with the true friend or dear, the case is quite the reverse; for that is proved to be dear because of the hated, and if the hated were away it would be no longer dear.'

'Very true,' he replied: 'at any rate not if our present view holds good.'

'But, oh! Will you tell me,' I said, 'whether if evil were to perish, we should hunger any more, or thirst any more, or have any similar desire? Or may we suppose that hunger will remain while men and animals remain, but not so as to be hurtful? And the same of thirst and the other desires, that they will remain, but will not be evil because evil has perished? Or rather shall I say, that to ask what either will be then or will not be is ridiculous, for who knows? This we do know, that in our present condition hunger may injure us, and may also benefit us: Is not that true?'

'Yes.'

'And in like manner thirst or any similar desire may sometimes be a good and sometimes an evil to us, and sometimes neither one nor the other?'

'To be sure.'

'But is there any reason why, because evil perishes, that which is not evil should perish with it?'

'None.'

'Then, even if evil perishes, the desires which are neither good nor evil will remain?'

'Clearly they will.'

'And must not a man love that which he desires and affects?'

'He must.'

'Then, even if evil perishes, there may still remain some elements of love or friendship?'

'Yes.'

'But not if evil is the cause of friendship: for in that case nothing will be the friend of any other thing after the destruction of evil; for the effect cannot remain when the cause is destroyed.'

'True.'

'And have we not admitted already that the friend loves something for a reason? and at the time of making the admission we were of opinion that the neither good nor evil loves the good because of the evil?'

'Very true.'

'But now our view is changed, and we conceive that there must be some other cause of friendship?'

'I suppose so.'

'May not the truth be rather, as we were saying just now, that desire is the cause of friendship; for that which desires is dear to that which is desired at the time of desiring it? And may not the other theory have been only a long story about nothing?'

'Likely enough.'

'But surely,' I said, 'he who desires, desires that of which he is in want?'

'Yes.'

'And that of which he is in want is dear to him?'

'True.'

'And he is in want of that of which he is deprived?'

'Certainly.'

'Then love, and desire, and friendship would appear to be of the natural or congenial. Such, Lysis and Menexenus, is the inference.'

They assented.

'Then if you are friends, you must have natures which are congenial to one another?'

'Certainly,' they both said.

'And I say, my boys, that no one who loves or desires another would ever have loved or desired or affected him, if he had not been in some way congenial to him, either in his soul, or in his character, or in his manners, or in his form.'

'Yes, yes,' said Menexenus. But Lysis was silent.

'Then,' I said, 'the conclusion is, that what is of a congenial nature must be loved.'

'It follows,' he said.

'Then the lover, who is true and no counterfeit, must of necessity be loved by his love.'

Lysis and Menexenus gave a faint assent to this; and Hippothales changed into all manner of colours with delight.

Here, intending to revise the argument, I said: 'Can we point out any difference between the congenial and the like? For if that is possible, then I think, Lysis and Menexenus, there may be some sense in our argument about friendship. But if the congenial is only the like, how will you get rid of the other argument, of the uselessness of like to like in as far as they are like; for to say that what is useless is dear, would be absurd? Suppose, then, that we agree to distinguish between the congenial and the like—in the intoxication of argument, that may perhaps be allowed.'

'Very true.'

'And shall we further say that the good is congenial, and the evil uncongenial to everyone? Or again that the evil is congenial to the evil, and the good to the good; and that which is neither good nor evil to that which is neither good nor evil?'

They agreed to the latter alternative.

'Then, my boys, we have again fallen into the old discarded error; for the unjust will be the friend of the unjust, and the bad of the bad, as well as the good of the good.'

'That appears to be the result.'

'But again, if we say that the congenial is the same as the good, in that case the good and he only will be the friend of the good.'

'True.'

'But that too was a position of ours which, as you will remember, has been already refuted by ourselves.'

'We remember.'

'Then what is to be done? Or rather is there anything to be done? I can only, like the wise men who argue in courts, sum up the arguments: If neither the beloved, nor the lover, nor the like, nor the unlike, nor the good, nor the congenial, nor any other of whom we spoke—for there were such a number of them that I cannot remember all—if none of these are friends, I know not what remains to be said.'

Here I was going to invite the opinion of some older person, when suddenly we were interrupted by the tutors of Lysis and Menexenus, who came upon us like an evil apparition with their brothers, and bade them go home, as it was getting late. At first, we and the by-standers drove them off; but afterwards, as they would not mind, and only went on shouting in their barbarous dialect, and got angry, and kept calling the boys—they appeared to us to have been drinking rather too much at the Hermaea, which made them difficult to manage—we fairly gave way and broke up the company.

I said, however, a few words to the boys at parting: 'O Menexenus and Lysis, how ridiculous that you two boys, and I, an old boy, who would fain be one of you, should imagine ourselves to be friends—this is what the by standers will go away and say—and as yet we have not been able to discover what is a friend!'

LACHES

PERSONS OF THE DIALOGUE: Lysimachus, son of Aristides. Melesias, son of Thucydides. Their sons. Nicias, Laches, Socrates.

LYSIMACHUS: You have seen the exhibition of the man fighting in armor, Nicias and Laches, but we did not tell you at the time the reason why my friend Melesias and I asked you to go with us and see him. I think that we may as well confess what this was, for we certainly ought not to have any reserve with you. The reason was, that we were intending to ask your advice. Some laugh at the very notion of advising others, and when they are asked will not say what they think. They guess at the wishes of the person who asks them, and answer according to his, and not according to their own, opinion. But as we know that you are good judges, and will say exactly what you think, we have taken you into our counsels. The matter about which I am making all this preface is as follows: Melesias and I have two sons; that is his son, and he is named Thucydides, after his grandfather; and this is mine, who is also called after his grandfather, Aristides. Now, we are resolved to take the greatest care of the youths, and not to let them run about as they like, which is too often the way with the young, when they are no longer children, but to begin at once and do the utmost that we can for them. And knowing you to have sons of your own, we thought that you were most likely to have attended to their training and improvement, and, if perchance you have not attended to them, we may remind you that you ought to have done so, and would invite you to assist us in the fulfillment of a common duty. I will tell you, Nicias and Laches, even at the risk of being tedious, how we came to think of this. Melesias and I live together, and our sons live with us; and now, as I was saying at first, we are going to confess to you. Both of us often talk to the lads about the many noble deeds which our own fathers did in war and peace—in the management of the allies, and in the administration of the city; but neither of us has any deeds of his own which he can show. The truth is that we are ashamed of this contrast being seen by them, and we blame our fathers for letting us be spoiled in the days of our youth, while they were occupied with the concerns of others; and we urge all this upon the lads, pointing out to them that they will not grow up to honor if they are rebellious and take no pains about themselves; but that if they take pains they may, perhaps, become worthy of the names which they bear. They, on their part, promise to comply with our wishes; and our care is to discover what studies or pursuits are likely to be most improving to them. Someone commended to us the art of fighting in armor, which he thought an excellent accomplishment for a young man to learn; and he praised the man whose exhibition you have seen, and told us to go and see him. And we determined that we would go, and get you to accompany us; and we were intending at the same time, if you did not object, to take counsel with you about the education of our sons. That is the matter which we wanted to talk over with you; and we hope that you will give us your opinion about this art of fighting in armour, and about any other studies or pursuits which may or may not be desirable for a young man to learn. Please to say whether you agree to our proposal.

NICIAS: As far as I am concerned, Lysimachus and Melesias, I applaud your purpose, and will gladly assist you; and I believe that you, Laches, will be equally glad.

LACHES: Certainly, Nicias; and I quite approve of the remark which Lysimachus made about his own father and the father of Melesias, and which is applicable, not only to them, but to us, and to everyone who is occupied with public affairs. As he says, such persons are too apt to be negligent and careless of their own children and their private concerns. There is much truth in that remark of yours, Lysimachus. But why, instead of consulting us, do you not consult our friend Socrates about the education of the youths? He is of the same deme with you, and is always passing his time in places where the youth have any noble study or pursuit, such as you are inquiring after.

LYSIMACHUS: Why, Laches, has Socrates ever attended to matters of this sort?

LACHES: Certainly, Lysimachus.

NICIAS: That I have the means of knowing as well as Laches; for quite lately he supplied me with a teacher of music for my sons—Damon, the disciple of Agathocles, who is a most accomplished man in every way, as well as a musician, and a companion of inestimable value for young men at their age.

LYSIMACHUS: Those who have reached my time of life, Socrates and Nicias and Laches, fall out of acquaintance with the young, because they are generally detained at home by old age; but you, O son of Sophroniscus, should let your fellow demesman have the benefit of any advice which you are able to give. Moreover I have a claim upon you as an old friend of your father; for I and he were always companions and friends, and to the hour of his death there never was a difference between us; and now it comes back to me, at the mention of your name, that I have heard these lads talking to one another at home, and often speaking of Socrates in terms of the highest praise; but I have never thought to ask them whether the son of Sophroniscus was the person whom they meant. Tell me, my boys, whether this is the Socrates of whom you have often spoken?

SON: Certainly, father, this is he.

LYSIMACHUS: I am delighted to hear, Socrates, that you maintain the name of your father, who was a most excellent man; and I further rejoice at the prospect of our family ties being renewed.

LACHES: Indeed, Lysimachus, you ought not to give him up; for I can assure you that I have seen him maintaining, not only his father's, but also his country's name. He was my companion in the retreat from Delium, and I can tell you that if others had only been like him, the honor of our country would have been upheld, and the great defeat would never have occurred.

LACHES

LYSIMACHUS: That is very high praise which is accorded to you, Socrates, by faithful witnesses and for actions like those which they praise. Let me tell you the pleasure which I feel in hearing of your fame; and I hope that you will regard me as one of your warmest friends. You ought to have visited us long ago, and made yourself at home with us; but now, from this day forward, as we have at last found one another out, do as I say—come and make acquaintance with me, and with these young men, that I may continue your friend, as I was your father's. I shall expect you to do so, and shall venture at some future time to remind you of your duty. But what say you of the matter of which we were beginning to speak—the art of fighting in armor? Is that a practice in which the lads may be advantageously instructed?

SOCRATES: I will endeavour to advise you, Lysimachus, as far as I can in this matter, and also in every way will comply with your wishes; but as I am younger and not so experienced, I think that I ought certainly to hear first what my elders have to say, and to learn of them, and if I have anything to add, then I may venture to give my opinion to them as well as to you. Suppose, Nicias, that one or other of you begin.

NICIAS: I have no objection, Socrates; and my opinion is that the acquirement of this art is in many ways useful to young men. It is an advantage to them that among the favorite amusements of their leisure hours they should have one which tends to improve and not to injure their bodily health. No gymnastics could be better or harder exercise;

and this, and the art of riding, are of all arts most befitting to a freeman; for they only who are thus trained in the use of arms are the athletes of our military profession, trained in that on which the conflict turns. Moreover in actual battle, when you have to fight in a line with a number of others, such an acquirement will be of some use, and will be of the greatest whenever the ranks are broken and you have to fight singly, either in pursuit, when you are attacking someone who is defending himself, or in flight, when you have to defend yourself against an assailant. Certainly he who possessed the art could not meet with any harm at the hands of a single person, or perhaps of several; and in any case he would have a great advantage. Further, this sort of skill inclines a man to the love of other noble lessons; for every man who has learned how to fight in armour will desire to learn the proper arrangement of an army, which is the sequel of the lesson and when he has learned this, and his ambition is once fired, he will go on to learn the complete art of the general. There is no difficulty in seeing that the knowledge and practice of other military arts will be honourable and valuable to a man; and this lesson may be the beginning of them. Let me add a further advantage, which is by no means a slight one—that this science will make any man a great deal more valiant and self-possessed in the field. And I will not disdain to mention, what by some may be thought to be a small matter—he will make a better appearance at the right time; that is to say, at the time when his appearance will strike terror into his enemies. My opinion then, Lysimachus, is, as I say, that the youths should be instructed in this art, and for the reasons which I have given. But Laches may take a different view; and I shall be very glad to hear what he has to say.

LACHES: I should not like to maintain, Nicias, that any kind of knowledge is not to be learned; for all knowledge appears to be a good: and if, as Nicias and as the teachers of the art affirm, this use of arms is really a species of knowledge, then it ought to be learned; but if not, and if those who profess to teach it are deceivers only; or if it be knowledge, but not of a valuable sort, then what is the use of learning it? I say this, because I think that if it had been really valuable, the Lacedaemonians, whose whole life is passed in finding out and practising the arts which give them an advantage over other nations in war, would have discovered this one. And even if they had not, still these professors of the art would certainly not have failed to discover that of all the Hellenes the Lacedaemonians have the greatest interest in such matters, and that a master of the art who was honored among them would be sure to make his fortune among other nations, just as a tragic poet would who is honoured among ourselves; which is the reason why he who fancies that he can write a tragedy does not go about itinerating in the neighbouring states, but rushes hither straight, and exhibits at Athens; and this is natural. Whereas I perceive that these fighters in armor regard Lacedaemon as a sacred inviolable territory, which they do not touch with the point of their foot; but they make a circuit of the neighbouring states, and would rather exhibit to any others than to the Spartans; and particularly to those who would themselves acknowledge that they are by no means first rate in the arts of war. Further, Lysimachus, I have encountered a good many of these gentlemen in actual service, and have taken their measure, which I can give you at once; for none of these masters of fence have ever been distinguished in war—there has been a sort of fatality about them; while in all other arts the men of note have been always those who have practised the art, they appear to be a most unfortunate exception. For example, this very Stesilaus, whom you and I have just witnessed exhibiting in all that crowd and making such great professions of his powers, I have seen at another time making, in sober truth, an involuntary exhibition of himself, which was a far better spectacle. He was a marine on board a ship which struck a transport vessel, and was armed with a weapon, half spear, half scythe; the singularity of this weapon was worthy of the singularity of the man. To make a long story short, I will only tell you what happened to this notable invention of the scythe spear. He was fighting, and the scythe was caught in the rigging of the other ship, and stuck fast; and he tugged, but was unable to get his weapon free. The two ships were passing one another. He first ran along his own ship holding on to the spear; but as the other ship passed by and drew him after as he was holding on, he let the spear slip through his hand until he retained only the end of the handle. The people in the transport clapped their hands, and laughed at his ridiculous figure; and when someone threw a stone, which fell on the deck at his feet, and he quitted his hold of the scythe-spear, the crew of his own trireme also burst out laughing; they could not refrain when they beheld the weapon waving in the air, suspended from the transport. Now I do not deny that there may be something in such an art, as Nicias asserts, but I tell you my experience; and, as I said at first, whether this be an art of which the advantage is so slight, or not an art at all, but only an imposition, in either case such an acquirement is not worth having. For my opinion is, that if the professor of this art be a coward, he will be likely to become rash, and his character will be only more notorious; or if he be brave, and fail ever so little, other men will be on the watch, and he will be greatly traduced; for there is a jealousy of such pretenders; and unless a man be pre-eminent in valour, he cannot help being ridiculous, if he says that he has this sort of skill. Such is my judgment, Lysimachus, of the desirableness of this art; but, as I said at first, ask Socrates, and do not let him go until he has given you his opinion of the matter.

LYSIMACHUS: I am going to ask this favour of you, Socrates; as is the more necessary because the two councillors disagree, and someone is in a manner still needed who will decide between them. Had they agreed, no arbiter would have been required. But as Laches has voted one way and Nicias another, I should like to hear with which of our two friends you agree.

SOCRATES: What, Lysimachus, are you going to accept the opinion of the majority?

LYSIMACHUS: Why, yes, Socrates; what else am I to do?

SOCRATES: And would you do so too, Melesias? If you were deliberating about the gymnastic training of your son, would you follow the advice of the majority of us, or the opinion of the one who had been trained and exercised under a skillful master?

MELESIAS: The latter, Socrates; as would surely be reasonable.

SOCRATES: His one vote would be worth more than the vote of all us four?

MELESIAS: Certainly.

SOCRATES: And for this reason, as I imagine—because a good decision is based on knowledge and not on numbers?

MELESIAS: To be sure.

SOCRATES: Must we not then first of all ask, whether there is any one of us who has knowledge of that about which we are deliberating? If there is, let us take his advice, though he be one only, and not mind the rest; if there is not, let us seek further counsel. Is this a slight matter about which you and Lysimachus are deliberating? Are you not risking the greatest of your possessions? For children are your riches; and upon their turning out well or ill depends the whole order of their father's house.

MELESIAS: That is true.

SOCRATES: Great care, then, is required in this matter?

MELESIAS: Certainly.

SOCRATES: Suppose, as I was just now saying, that we were considering, or wanting to consider, who was the best trainer. Should we not select him who knew and had practised the art, and had the best teachers?

MELESIAS: I think that we should.

SOCRATES: But would there not arise a prior question about the nature of the art of which we want to find the masters?

MELESIAS: I do not understand.

SOCRATES: Let me try to make my meaning plainer then. I do not think that we have as yet decided what that is about which we are consulting, when we ask which of us is or is not skilled in the art, and has or has not had a teacher of the art.

NICIAS: Why, Socrates, is not the question whether young men ought or ought not to learn the art of fighting in armour?

SOCRATES: Yes, Nicias; but there is also a prior question, which I may illustrate in this way: When a person considers about applying a medicine to the eyes, would you say that he is consulting about the medicine or about the eyes?

NICIAS: About the eyes.

SOCRATES: And when he considers whether he shall set a bridle on a horse and at what time, he is thinking of the horse and not of the bridle?

NICIAS: True.

SOCRATES: And in a word, when he considers anything for the sake of another thing, he thinks of the end and not of the means?

NICIAS: Certainly.

SOCRATES: And when you call in an adviser, you should see whether he too is skillful in the accomplishment of the end which you have in view?

NICIAS: Most true.

SOCRATES: And at present we have in view some knowledge, of which the end is the soul of youth?

NICIAS: Yes.

SOCRATES: And we are inquiring, which of us is skillful or successful in the treatment of the soul, and which of us has had good teachers?

LACHES: Well but, Socrates; did you never observe that some persons, who have had no teachers, are more skillful than those who have, in some things?

SOCRATES: Yes, Laches, I have observed that; but you would not be very willing to trust them if they only professed to be masters of their art, unless they could show some proof of their skill or excellence in one or more works.

LACHES: That is true.

SOCRATES: And therefore, Laches and Nicias, as Lysimachus and Melesias, in their anxiety to improve the minds of their sons, have asked our advice about them, we too should tell them who our teachers were, if we say that we have had any, and prove them to be in the first place men of merit and experienced trainers of the minds of youth and also to have been really our teachers. Or if any of us says that he has no teacher, but that he has works of his own to show; then he should point out to them what Athenians or strangers, bond or free, he is generally acknowledged to have improved. But if he can show neither teachers nor works, then he should tell them to look out for others; and not run the risk of spoiling the children of friends, and thereby incurring the most formidable accusation which can be brought against anyone by those nearest to him. As for myself, Lysimachus and Melesias, I am the first to confess that I have never had a teacher of the art of virtue; although I have always from my earliest youth desired to have one. But I am too poor to give money to the Sophists, who are the only professors of moral improvement; and to this day I have never been able to discover the art myself, though I should not be surprised if Nicias or Laches may have discovered or learned it; for they are far wealthier than I am, and may therefore have learnt of others. And they are older too; so that they have had more time to make the discovery. And I really believe that they are able to educate a man; for unless they had been confident in their own knowledge, they would never have spoken thus decidedly of the pursuits which are advantageous or hurtful to a young man. I repose confidence in both of them; but I am surprised to find that they differ from one another. And therefore, Lysimachus, as Laches suggested that you should detain me, and not let me go until I answered, I in turn earnestly beseech and advise you to detain Laches and Nicias, and question them. I would have you say to them: Socrates avers that he has no knowledge of the matter—he is unable to decide which of you speaks truly; neither discoverer nor student is he of anything of the kind. But you, Laches and Nicias, should each of you tell us who is the most skillful educator whom you have ever known; and whether you invented the art yourselves, or learned of another; and if you learned, who were your respective teachers, and who were their brothers in the art; and then, if you are too much occupied in politics to teach us yourselves, let us go to them, and present them with gifts, or make interest with them, or both, in the hope that they may be induced to take charge of our children and of yours; and then they will not grow up inferior, and disgrace their ancestors. But if you are yourselves original discoverers in that field, give us some proof of your skill. Who are they who, having been inferior persons, have become under your care good and noble? For if this is your first attempt at education, there is a danger that you may be trying the experiment, not on the 'vile corpus' of a Carian slave, but on your own sons, or the sons of your friend, and, as the proverb says, 'break the large vessel in learning to make pots.' Tell us then, what qualities you claim or do not claim. Make them tell you that, Lysimachus, and do not let them off.

LYSIMACHUS: I very much approve of the words of Socrates, my friends; but you, Nicias and Laches, must determine whether you will be questioned, and give an explanation about matters of this sort. Assuredly, I and Melesias would be greatly pleased to hear you answer the questions which Socrates asks, if you will: for I began by saying that we took you into our counsels because we thought that you would have attended to the subject, especially as you have children who, like our own, are nearly of an age to be educated. Well, then, if you have no objection, suppose that you take Socrates into partnership; and do you and he ask and answer one another's questions: for, as he has well said, we are deliberating about the most important of our concerns. I hope that you will see fit to comply with our request.

NICIAS: I see very clearly, Lysimachus, that you have only known Socrates' father, and have no acquaintance with Socrates himself: at least, you can only have known him when he was a child, and may have met him among his fellow-wardsmen, in company with his father, at a sacrifice, or at some other gathering. You clearly show that you have never known him since he arrived at manhood.

LYSIMACHUS: Why do you say that, Nicias?

NICIAS: Because you seem not to be aware that anyone who has an intellectual affinity to Socrates and enters into conversation with him is liable to be drawn into an argument; and whatever subject he may start, he will be continually carried round and round by him, until at last he finds that he has to give an account both of his present and past life; and when he is once entangled, Socrates will not let him go until he has completely and thoroughly sifted him. Now I am used to his ways; and I know that he will certainly do as I say, and also that I myself shall be the sufferer; for I am fond of his conversation, Lysimachus. And I think that there is no harm in being reminded of any wrong thing which we are, or have been, doing: he who does not fly from reproof will be sure to take more heed of his after-life; as Solon says, he will wish and desire to be learning so long as he lives, and will not think that old age of itself brings wisdom. To me, to be cross-examined by Socrates is neither unusual nor unpleasant; indeed, I knew all along that where Socrates was, the argument would soon pass from our sons to ourselves; and therefore, I say that for my part, I am quite willing to discourse with Socrates in his own manner; but you had better ask our friend Laches what his feeling may be.

LACHES: I have but one feeling, Nicias, or (shall I say?) two feelings, about discussions. Some would think that I am a lover, and to others I may seem to be a hater of discourse; for when I hear a man discoursing of virtue, or of any sort of wisdom, who is a true man and worthy of his theme, I am delighted beyond measure: and I compare the man and his words, and note the harmony and correspondence of them. And such a one I deem to be the true musician, attuned to a fairer harmony than that of the lyre, or any pleasant instrument of music; for truly he has in his own life a harmony of words and deeds arranged, not in the Ionian, or in the Phrygian mode, nor yet in the Lydian, but in the true Hellenic mode, which is the Dorian, and no other. Such a one makes me merry with the sound of his voice; and when I hear him I am thought to be a lover of discourse; so eager am I in drinking in his words. But a man whose actions do not agree with his words is an annoyance to me; and the better he speaks the more I hate him, and then I seem to be a hater of discourse. As to Socrates, I have no knowledge of his words, but of old, as would seem, I have had experience of his deeds; and his deeds show that free and noble sentiments are natural to him. And if his words accord, then I am of one mind with him, and shall be delighted to be interrogated by a man such as he is, and shall not be annoyed at having to learn of him: for I too agree with Solon, 'that I would fain grow old, learning many things.' But I must be allowed to add 'of the good only.' Socrates must be willing to allow that he is a good teacher, or I shall be a dull and uncongenial pupil: but that the teacher is younger, or not as yet in repute—anything of that sort is of no account with me. And therefore, Socrates, I give you notice that you may teach and confute me as much as ever you like, and also learn of me anything which I know. So high is the opinion which I have entertained of you ever since the day on which you were my companion in danger, and gave a proof of your valour such as only the man of merit can give. Therefore, say whatever you like, and do not mind about the difference of our ages.

SOCRATES: I cannot say that either of you show any reluctance to take counsel and advise with me.

LYSIMACHUS: But this is our proper business; and yours as well as ours, for I reckon you as one of us. Please then to take my place, and find out from Nicias and Laches what we want to know, for the sake of the youths, and talk and consult with them: for I am old, and my memory is bad; and I do not remember the questions which I am going to ask, or the answers to them; and if there is any interruption I am quite lost. I will therefore beg of you to carry on the proposed discussion by your selves; and I will listen, and Melesias and I will act upon your conclusions.

SOCRATES: Let us, Nicias and Laches, comply with the request of Lysimachus and Melesias. There will be no harm in asking ourselves the question which was first proposed to us: 'Who have been our own instructors in this sort of training, and whom have we made better?' But the other mode of carrying on the inquiry will bring us equally to the same point, and will be more like proceeding from first principles. For if we knew that the addition of something would improve some other thing, and were able to make the addition, then, clearly, we must know how that about which we are advising may be best and most easily attained. Perhaps you do not understand what I mean. Then let me make my meaning plainer in this way. Suppose we knew that the addition of sight makes better the eyes which possess this gift, and also were able to impart sight to the eyes, then, clearly, we should know the nature of sight, and should be able to advise how this gift of sight may be best and most easily attained; but if we knew neither what sight is, nor what hearing is, we should not be very good medical advisers about the eyes or the ears, or about the best mode of giving sight and hearing to them.

LACHES: That is true, Socrates.

SOCRATES: And are not our two friends, Laches, at this very moment inviting us to consider in what way the gift of virtue may be imparted to their sons for the improvement of their minds?

LACHES: Very true.

SOCRATES: Then must we not first know the nature of virtue? For how can we advise anyone about the best mode of attaining something of which we are wholly ignorant?

LACHES: I do not think that we can, Socrates.

SOCRATES: Then, Laches, we may presume that we know the nature of virtue?

LACHES: Yes.

SOCRATES: And that which we know we must surely be able to tell?

LACHES: Certainly.

SOCRATES: I would not have us begin, my friend, with inquiring about the whole of virtue; for that may be more than we can accomplish; let us first consider whether we have a sufficient knowledge of a part; the inquiry will thus probably be made easier to us.

LACHES: Let us do as you say, Socrates.

SOCRATES: Then which of the parts of virtue shall we select? Must we not select that to which the art of fighting in armor is supposed to conduce? And is not that generally thought to be courage?

LACHES: Yes, certainly.

SOCRATES: Then, Laches, suppose that we first set about determining the nature of courage, and in the second place proceed to inquire how the young men may attain this quality by the help of studies and pursuits. Tell me, if you can, what is courage.

LACHES: Indeed, Socrates, I see no difficulty in answering; he is a man of courage who does not run away, but remains at his post and fights against the enemy; there can be no mistake about that.

SOCRATES: Very good, Laches; and yet I fear that I did not express myself clearly; and therefore you have answered not the question which I intended to ask, but another.

LACHES: What do you mean, Socrates?

SOCRATES: I will endeavour to explain; you would call a man courageous who remains at his post, and fights with the enemy?

LACHES: Certainly I should.

SOCRATES: And so should I; but what would you say of another man, who fights flying, instead of remaining?

LACHES: How flying?

SOCRATES: Why, as the Scythians are said to fight, flying as well as pursuing; and as Homer says in praise of the horses of Aeneas, that they knew 'how to pursue, and fly quickly hither and thither'; and he passes an encomium on Aeneas himself, as having a knowledge of fear or flight, and calls him 'an author of fear or flight.'

LACHES: Yes, Socrates, and there Homer is right: for he was speaking of chariots, as you were speaking of the Scythian cavalry, who have that way of fighting; but the heavy-armed Greek fights, as I say, remaining in his rank.

SOCRATES: And yet, Laches, you must except the Lacedaemonians at Plataea, who, when they came upon the light shields of the Persians, are said not to have been willing to stand and fight, and to have fled; but when the ranks of the Persians were broken, they turned upon them like cavalry, and won the battle of Plataea.

LACHES: That is true.

SOCRATES: That was my meaning when I said that I was to blame in having put my question badly, and that this was the reason of your answering badly. For I meant to ask you not only about the courage of heavy-armed soldiers, but about the courage of cavalry and every other style of soldier; and not only who are courageous in war, but who are courageous in perils by sea, and who in disease, or in poverty, or again in politics, are courageous; and not only who are courageous against pain or fear, but mighty to contend against desires and pleasures, either fixed in their rank or turning upon their enemy. There is this sort of courage—is there not, Laches?

LACHES: Certainly, Socrates.

SOCRATES: And all these are courageous, but some have courage in pleasures, and some in pains: some in desires, and some in fears, and some are cowards under the same conditions, as I should imagine.

LACHES: Very true.

SOCRATES: Now I was asking about courage and cowardice in general. And I will begin with courage, and once more ask, what is that common quality, which is the same in all these cases, and which is called courage? Do you now understand what I mean?

LACHES: Not over well.

SOCRATES: I mean this: As I might ask what is that quality which is called quickness, and which is found in running, in playing the lyre, in speaking, in learning, and in many other similar actions, or rather which we possess in nearly every action that is worth mentioning of arms, legs, mouth, voice, mind—would you not apply the term quickness to all of them?

LACHES: Quite true.

SOCRATES: And suppose I were to be asked by someone: What is that common quality, Socrates, which, in all these uses of the word, you call quickness? I should say the quality which accomplishes much in a little time—whether in running, speaking, or in any other sort of action.

LACHES: You would be quite correct.

SOCRATES: And now, Laches, do you try and tell me in like manner, what is that common quality which is called courage, and which includes all the various uses of the term when applied both to pleasure and pain, and in all the cases to which I was just now referring?

LACHES: I should say that courage is a sort of endurance of the soul, if I am to speak of the universal nature which pervades them all.

SOCRATES: But that is what we must do if we are to answer the question. And yet I cannot say that every kind of endurance is, in my opinion, to be deemed courage. Hear my reason: I am sure, Laches, that you would consider courage to be a very noble quality.

LACHES: Most noble, certainly.

SOCRATES: And you would say that a wise endurance is also good and noble?

LACHES: Very noble.

SOCRATES: But what would you say of a foolish endurance? Is not that, on the other hand, to be regarded as evil and hurtful?

LACHES: True.

SOCRATES: And is anything noble which is evil and hurtful?

LACHES: I ought not to say that, Socrates.

SOCRATES: Then you would not admit that sort of endurance to be courage—for it is not noble, but courage is noble?

LACHES: You are right.

SOCRATES: Then, according to you, only the wise endurance is courage?

LACHES: True.

SOCRATES: But as to the epithet 'wise,'—wise in what? In all things small as well as great? For example, if a man shows the quality of endurance in spending his money wisely, knowing that by spending he will acquire more in the end, do you call him courageous?

LACHES: Assuredly not.

SOCRATES: Or, for example, if a man is a physician, and his son, or some patient of his, has inflammation of the lungs, and begs that he may be allowed to eat or drink something, and the other is firm and refuses; is that courage?

LACHES: No; that is not courage at all, any more than the last.

SOCRATES: Again, take the case of one who endures in war, and is willing to fight, and wisely calculates and knows that others will help him, and that there will be fewer and inferior men against him than there are with him; and suppose that he has also advantages of position; would you say of such a one who endures with all this wisdom and preparation, that he, or some man in the opposing army who is in the opposite circumstances to these and yet endures and remains at his post, is the braver?

LACHES: I should say that the latter, Socrates, was the braver.

SOCRATES: But, surely, this is a foolish endurance in comparison with the other?

LACHES: That is true.

SOCRATES: Then you would say that he who in an engagement of cavalry endures, having the knowledge of horsemanship, is not so courageous as he who endures, having no such knowledge?

LACHES: So I should say.

SOCRATES: And he who endures, having a knowledge of the use of the sling, or the bow, or of any other art, is not so courageous as he who endures, not having such a knowledge?

LACHES: True.

SOCRATES: And he who descends into a well, and dives, and holds out in this or any similar action, having no knowledge of diving, or the like, is, as you would say, more courageous than those who have this knowledge?

LACHES: Why, Socrates, what else can a man say?

SOCRATES: Nothing, if that be what he thinks.

LACHES: But that is what I do think.

SOCRATES: And yet men who thus run risks and endure are foolish, Laches, in comparison of those who do the same things, having the skill to do them.

LACHES: That is true.

SOCRATES: But foolish boldness and endurance appeared before to be base and hurtful to us.

LACHES: Quite true.

SOCRATES: Whereas courage was acknowledged to be a noble quality.

LACHES: True.

SOCRATES: And now on the contrary we are saying that the foolish endurance, which was before held in dishonour, is courage.

LACHES: Very true.

SOCRATES: And are we right in saying so?

LACHES: Indeed, Socrates, I am sure that we are not right.

SOCRATES: Then according to your statement, you and I, Laches, are not attuned to the Dorian mode, which is a harmony of words and deeds; for our deeds are not in accordance with our words. Anyone would say that we had courage who saw us in action, but not, I imagine, he who heard us talking about courage just now.

LACHES: That is most true.

LACHES

SOCRATES: And is this condition of ours satisfactory?

LACHES: Quite the reverse.

SOCRATES: Suppose, however, that we admit the principle of which we are speaking to a certain extent.

LACHES: To what extent and what principle do you mean?

SOCRATES: The principle of endurance. We too must endure and persevere in the inquiry, and then courage will not laugh at our faint-heartedness in searching for courage; which after all may, very likely, be endurance.

LACHES: I am ready to go on, Socrates; and yet I am unused to investigations of this sort. But the spirit of controversy has been aroused in me by what has been said; and I am really grieved at being thus unable to express my meaning. For I fancy that I do know the nature of courage; but, somehow or other, she has slipped away from me, and I cannot get hold of her and tell her nature.

SOCRATES: But, my dear friend, should not the good sportsman follow the track, and not be lazy?

LACHES: Certainly, he should.

SOCRATES: And shall we invite Nicias to join us? He may be better at the sport than we are. What do you say?

LACHES: I should like that.

SOCRATES: Come then, Nicias, and do what you can to help your friends, who are tossing on the waves of argument, and at the last gasp: you see our extremity, and may save us and also settle your own opinion, if you will tell us what you think about courage.

NICIAS: I have been thinking, Socrates, that you and Laches are not defining courage in the right way; for you have forgotten an excellent saying which I have heard from your own lips.

SOCRATES: What is it, Nicias?

NICIAS: I have often heard you say that 'Every man is good in that in which he is wise, and bad in that in which he is unwise.'

SOCRATES: That is certainly true, Nicias.

NICIAS: And therefore if the brave man is good, he is also wise.

SOCRATES: Do you hear him, Laches?

LACHES: Yes, I hear him, but I do not very well understand him.

SOCRATES: I think that I understand him; and he appears to me to mean that courage is a sort of wisdom.

LACHES: What can he possibly mean, Socrates?

SOCRATES: That is a question which you must ask of himself.

LACHES: Yes.

LACHES

SOCRATES: Tell him then, Nicias, what you mean by this wisdom; for you surely do not mean the wisdom which plays the flute?

NICIAS: Certainly not.

SOCRATES: Nor the wisdom which plays the lyre?

NICIAS: No.

SOCRATES: But what is this knowledge then, and of what?

LACHES: I think that you put the question to him very well, Socrates; and I would like him to say what is the nature of this knowledge or wisdom.

NICIAS: I mean to say, Laches, that courage is the knowledge of that which inspires fear or confidence in war, or in anything.

LACHES: How strangely he is talking, Socrates.

SOCRATES: Why do you say so, Laches?

LACHES: Why, surely courage is one thing, and wisdom another.

SOCRATES: That is just what Nicias denies.

LACHES: Yes, that is what he denies; but he is so silly.

SOCRATES: Suppose that we instruct instead of abusing him?

NICIAS: Laches does not want to instruct me, Socrates; but having been proved to be talking nonsense himself, he wants to prove that I have been doing the same.

LACHES: Very true, Nicias; and you are talking nonsense, as I shall endeavour to show. Let me ask you a question: Do not physicians know the dangers of disease? Or do the courageous know them? Or are the physicians the same as the courageous?

NICIAS: Not at all.

LACHES: No more than the husbandmen who know the dangers of husbandry, or than other craftsmen, who have a knowledge of that which inspires them with fear or confidence in their own arts, and yet they are not courageous a whit the more for that.

SOCRATES: What is Laches saying, Nicias? He appears to be saying something of importance.

NICIAS: Yes, he is saying something, but it is not true.

SOCRATES: How so?

NICIAS: Why, because he does not see that the physician's knowledge only extends to the nature of health and disease: he can tell the sick man no more than this. Do you imagine, Laches, that the physician knows whether health or disease is the more terrible to a man? Had not many a man better never get up from a sick bed? I should like to know whether you think that life is always better than death. May not death often be the better of the two?

LACHES

LACHES: Yes, certainly so in my opinion.

NICIAS: And do you think that the same things are terrible to those who had better die, and to those who had better live?

LACHES: Certainly not.

NICIAS: And do you suppose that the physician or any other artist knows this, or anyone indeed, except he who is skilled in the grounds of fear and hope? And him I call the courageous.

SOCRATES: Do you understand his meaning, Laches?

LACHES: Yes; I suppose that, in his way of speaking, the soothsayers are courageous. For who but one of them can know to whom to die or to live is better? And yet Nicias, would you allow that you are yourself a soothsayer, or are you neither a soothsayer nor courageous?

NICIAS: What! Do you mean to say that the soothsayer ought to know the grounds of hope or fear?

LACHES: Indeed I do: who but he?

NICIAS: Much rather I should say he of whom I speak; for the soothsayer ought to know only the signs of things that are about to come to pass, whether death or disease, or loss of property, or victory, or defeat in war, or in any sort of contest; but to whom the suffering or not suffering of these things will be for the best, can no more be decided by the soothsayer than by one who is no soothsayer.

LACHES: I cannot understand what Nicias would be at, Socrates; for he represents the courageous man as neither a soothsayer, nor a physician, nor in any other character, unless he means to say that he is a god. My opinion is that he does not like honestly to confess that he is talking nonsense, but that he shuffles up and down in order to conceal the difficulty into which he has got himself. You and I, Socrates, might have practised a similar shuffle just now, if we had only wanted to avoid the appearance of inconsistency. And if we had been arguing in a court of law there might have been reason in so doing; but why should a man deck himself out with vain words at a meeting of friends such as this?

SOCRATES: I quite agree with you, Laches, that he should not. But perhaps Nicias is serious, and not merely talking for the sake of talking. Let us ask him just to explain what he means, and if he has reason on his side we will agree with him; if not, we will instruct him.

LACHES: Do you, Socrates, if you like, ask him: I think that I have asked enough.

SOCRATES: I do not see why I should not; and my question will do for both of us.

LACHES: Very good.

SOCRATES: Then tell me, Nicias, or rather tell us, for Laches and I are partners in the argument: Do you mean to affirm that courage is the knowledge of the grounds of hope and fear?

NICIAS: I do.

SOCRATES: And not every man has this knowledge; the physician and the soothsayer have it not; and they will not be courageous unless they acquire it—that is what you were saying?

NICIAS: I was.

SOCRATES: Then this is certainly not a thing which every pig would know, as the proverb says, and therefore he could not be courageous.

NICIAS: I think not.

SOCRATES: Clearly not, Nicias; not even such a big pig as the Crommyonian sow would be called by you courageous. And this I say not as a joke, but because I think that he who assents to your doctrine, that courage is the knowledge of the grounds of fear and hope, cannot allow that any wild beast is courageous, unless he admits that a lion, or a leopard, or perhaps a boar, or any other animal, has such a degree of wisdom that he knows things which but a few human beings ever know by reason of their difficulty. He who takes your view of courage must affirm that a lion, and a stag, and a bull, and a monkey, have equally little pretensions to courage.

LACHES: Capital, Socrates; by the gods, that is truly good. And I hope, Nicias, that you will tell us whether these animals, which we all admit to be courageous, are really wiser than mankind; or whether you will have the boldness, in the face of universal opinion, to deny their courage.

NICIAS: Why, Laches, I do not call animals or any other things which have no fear of dangers, because they are ignorant of them, courageous, but only fearless and senseless. Do you imagine that I should call little children courageous, which fear no dangers because they know none? There is a difference, to my way of thinking, between fearlessness and courage. I am of opinion that thoughtful courage is a quality possessed by very few, but that rashness and boldness, and fearlessness, which has no forethought, are very common qualities possessed by many men, many women, many children, many animals. And you, and men in general, call by the term 'courageous' actions which I call rash—my courageous actions are wise actions.

LACHES: Behold, Socrates, how admirably, as he thinks, he dresses himself out in words, while seeking to deprive of the honor of courage those whom all the world acknowledges to be courageous.

NICIAS: Not so, Laches, but do not be alarmed; for I am quite willing to say of you and also of Lamachus, and of many other Athenians, that you are courageous and therefore wise.

LACHES: I could answer that; but I would not have you cast in my teeth that I am a haughty Aexonian.

SOCRATES: Do not answer him, Laches; I rather fancy that you are not aware of the source from which his wisdom is derived. He has got all this from my friend Damon, and Damon is always with Prodicus, who, of all the Sophists, is considered to be the best puller to pieces of words of this sort.

LACHES: Yes, Socrates; and the examination of such niceties is a much more suitable employment for a Sophist than for a great statesman whom the city chooses to preside over her.

SOCRATES: Yes, my sweet friend, but a great statesman is likely to have a great intelligence. And I think that the view which is implied in Nicias' definition of courage is worthy of examination.

LACHES: Then examine for yourself, Socrates.

SOCRATES: That is what I am going to do, my dear friend. Do not, however, suppose I shall let you out of the partnership; for I shall expect you to apply your mind, and join with me in the consideration of the question.

LACHES: I will if you think that I ought.

SOCRATES: Yes, I do; but I must beg of you, Nicias, to begin again. You remember that we originally considered courage to be a part of virtue.

NICIAS: Very true.

SOCRATES: And you yourself said that it was a part; and there were many other parts, all of which taken together are called virtue.

NICIAS: Certainly.

SOCRATES: Do you agree with me about the parts? For I say that justice, temperance, and the like, are all of them parts of virtue as well as courage. Would you not say the same?

NICIAS: Certainly.

SOCRATES: Well then, so far we are agreed. And now let us proceed a step, and try to arrive at a similar agreement about the fearful and the hopeful: I do not want you to be thinking one thing and myself another. Let me then tell you my own opinion, and if I am wrong you shall set me right: in my opinion the terrible and the hopeful are the things which do or do not create fear, and fear is not of the present, nor of the past, but is of future and expected evil. Do you not agree to that, Laches?

LACHES: Yes, Socrates, entirely.

SOCRATES: That is my view, Nicias; the terrible things, as I should say, are the evils which are future; and the hopeful are the good or not evil things which are future. Do you or do you not agree with me?

NICIAS: I agree.

SOCRATES: And the knowledge of these things you call courage?

NICIAS: Precisely.

SOCRATES: And now let me see whether you agree with Laches and myself as to a third point.

NICIAS: What is that?

SOCRATES: I will tell you. He and I have a notion that there is not one knowledge or science of the past, another of the present, a third of what is likely to be best and what will be best in the future; but that of all three there is one science only: for example, there is one science of medicine which is concerned with the inspection of health equally in all times, present, past, and future; and one science of husbandry in like manner, which is concerned with the productions of the earth in all times. As to the art of the general, you yourselves will be my witnesses that he has an excellent foreknowledge of the future, and that he claims to be the master and not the servant of the soothsayer, because he knows better what is happening or is likely to happen in war: and accordingly the law places the soothsayer under the general, and not the general under the soothsayer. Am I not correct in saying so, Laches?

LACHES: Quite correct.

SOCRATES: And do you, Nicias, also acknowledge that the same science has understanding of the same things, whether future, present, or past?

NICIAS: Yes, indeed Socrates; that is my opinion.

SOCRATES: And courage, my friend, is, as you say, a knowledge of the fearful and of the hopeful?

NICIAS: Yes.

SOCRATES: And the fearful, and the hopeful, are admitted to be future goods and future evils?

NICIAS: True.

SOCRATES: And the same science has to do with the same things in the future or at any time?

NICIAS: That is true.

SOCRATES: Then courage is not the science which is concerned with the fearful and hopeful, for they are future only; courage, like the other sciences, is concerned not only with good and evil of the future, but of the present and past, and of any time?

NICIAS: That, as I suppose, is true.

SOCRATES: Then the answer which you have given, Nicias, includes only a third part of courage; but our question extended to the whole nature of courage: and according to your view, that is, according to your present view, courage is not only the knowledge of the hopeful and the fearful, but seems to include nearly every good and evil without reference to time. What do you say to that alteration in your statement?

NICIAS: I agree, Socrates.

SOCRATES: But then, my dear friend, if a man knew all good and evil, and how they are, and have been, and will be produced, would he not be perfect, and wanting in no virtue, whether justice, or temperance, or holiness? He would possess them all, and he would know which were dangers and which were not, and guard against them whether they were supernatural or natural; and he would provide the good, as he would know how to deal both with gods or men.

NICIAS: I think, Socrates, that there is a great deal of truth in what you say.

SOCRATES: But then, Nicias, courage, according to this new definition of yours, instead of being a part of virtue only, will be all virtue?

NICIAS: It would seem so.

SOCRATES: But we were saying that courage is one of the parts of virtue?

NICIAS: Yes, that was what we were saying.

SOCRATES: And that is in contradiction with our present view?

NICIAS: That appears to be the case.

SOCRATES: Then, Nicias, we have not discovered what courage is.

NICIAS: We have not.

LACHES: And yet, friend Nicias, I imagined that you would have made the discovery, when you were so contemptuous of the answers which I made to Socrates. I had very great hopes that you would have been enlightened by the wisdom of Damon.

NICIAS: I perceive, Laches, that you think nothing of having displayed your ignorance of the nature of courage, but you look only to see whether I have not made a similar display; and if we are both equally ignorant of the things which a man who is good for anything should know, that, I suppose, will be of no consequence. You certainly appear to me very like the rest of the world, looking at your neighbor and not at yourself. I am of opinion that enough has been said on the subject which we have been discussing; and if anything has been imperfectly said, that may be hereafter corrected by the help of Damon, whom you think to laugh down, although you have never seen him, and with the help of others. And when I am satisfied myself, I will freely impart my satisfaction to you, for I think that you are very much in want of knowledge.

LACHES: You are a philosopher, Nicias; of that I am aware: nevertheless I would recommend Lysimachus and Melesias not to take you and me as advisers about the education of their children; but, as I said at first, they should ask Socrates and not let him off; if my own sons were old enough, I would have asked him myself.

NICIAS: To that I quite agree, if Socrates is willing to take them under his charge. I should not wish for any one else to be the tutor of Niceratus. But I observe that when I mention the matter to him he recommends to me some other tutor and refuses himself. Perhaps he may be more ready to listen to you, Lysimachus.

LYSIMACHUS: He ought, for certainly I would do things for him which I would not do for many others. What do you say, Socrates—will you comply? And are you ready to give assistance in the improvement of the youths?

SOCRATES: Indeed, Lysimachus, I should be very wrong in refusing to aid in the improvement of anybody. And if I had shown in this conversation that I had a knowledge which Nicias and Laches have not, then I admit that you would be right in inviting me to perform this duty; but as we are all in the same perplexity, why should one of us be preferred to another? I certainly think that no one should; and under these circumstances, let me offer you a piece of advice (and this need not go further than ourselves). I maintain, my friends, that every one of us should seek out the best teacher whom he can find, first for ourselves, who are greatly in need of one, and then for the youth, regardless of expense or anything. But I cannot advise that we remain as we are. And if any one laughs at us for going to school at our age, I would quote to them the authority of Homer, who says, that 'Modesty is not good for a needy man.' Let us then, regardless of what may be said of us, make the education of the youths our own education.

LYSIMACHUS: I like your proposal, Socrates; and as I am the oldest, I am also the most eager to go to school with the boys. Let me beg a favour of you: Come to my house to-morrow at dawn, and we will advise about these matters. For the present, let us make an end of the conversation.

SOCRATES: I will come to you tomorrow, Lysimachus, as you propose, God willing.

CHARMIDES

PERSONS OF THE DIALOGUE: Socrates, who is the narrator, Charmides, Chaerephon, Critias.
SCENE: The Palaestra of Taureas, which is near the Porch of the King Archon.

Yesterday evening I returned from the army at Potidaea, and having been a good while away, I thought that I should like to go and look at my old haunts. So I went into the palaestra of Taureas, which is over against the temple adjoining the porch of the King Archon, and there I found a number of persons, most of whom I knew, but not all.

My visit was unexpected, and no sooner did they see me entering than they saluted me from afar on all sides; and Chaerephon, who is a kind of madman, started up and ran to me, seizing my hand, and saying, 'How did you escape, Socrates?'—(I should explain that an engagement had taken place at Potidaea not long before we came away, of which the news had only just reached Athens.)'

'You see,' I replied, 'that here I am.'

'There was a report,' he said, 'that the engagement was very severe, and that many of our acquaintance had fallen.'

'That,' I replied, 'was not far from the truth.'

'I suppose,' he said, 'that you were present.'

'I was.'

'Then sit down, and tell us the whole story, which as yet we have only heard imperfectly.'

I took the place which he assigned to me, by the side of Critias the son of Callaeschrus, and when I had saluted him and the rest of the company, I told them the news from the army, and answered their several enquiries.

Then, when there had been enough of this, I, in my turn, began to make enquiries about matters at home—about the present state of philosophy, and about the youth.

I asked whether any of them were remarkable for wisdom or beauty, or both.

Critias, glancing at the door, invited my attention to some youths who were coming in, and talking noisily to one another, followed by a crowd.

'Of the beauties, Socrates,' he said, 'I fancy that you will soon be able to form a judgment.' For those who are just entering are the advanced guard of the great beauty, as he is thought to be, of the day, and he is likely to be not far off himself.'

'Who is he,' I said; 'and who is his father?'

'Charmides,' he replied, 'is his name; he is my cousin, and the son of my uncle Glaucon: I rather think that you know him too, although he was not grown up at the time of your departure.'

'Certainly, I know him,' I said, 'for he was remarkable even then when he was still a child, and I should imagine that by this time he must be almost a young man.'

'You will see,' he said, 'in a moment what progress he has made and what he is like.'

CHARMIDES

He had scarcely said the word, when Charmides entered.

Now you know, my friend, that I cannot measure anything, and of the beautiful, I am simply such a measure as a white line is of chalk; for almost all young persons appear to be beautiful in my eyes.

But at that moment, when I saw him coming in, I confess that I was quite astonished at his beauty and stature; all the world seemed to be enamoured of him; amazement and confusion reigned when he entered; and a troop of lovers followed him.

That grown-up men like ourselves should have been affected in this way was not surprising, but I observed that there was the same feeling among the boys; all of them, down to the very least child, turned and looked at him, as if he had been a statue.

Chaerephon called me and said: 'What do you think of him, Socrates? Has he not a beautiful face?'

'Most beautiful,' I said.

'But you would think nothing of his face,' he replied, 'if you could see his naked form: he is absolutely perfect.'

And to this they all agreed.

'By Heracles,' I said, 'there never was such a paragon, if he has only one other slight addition.'

'What is that?' said Critias.

'If he has a noble soul; and being of your house, Critias, he may be expected to have this.'

'He is as fair and good within, as he is without,' replied Critias.

'Then, before we see his body, should we not ask him to show us his soul, naked and undisguised? He is just of an age at which he will like to talk.'

'That he will,' said Critias, 'and I can tell you that he is a philosopher already, and also a considerable poet, not in his own opinion only, but in that of others.'

'That, my dear Critias,' I replied, 'is a distinction which has long been in your family, and is inherited by you from Solon. But why do you not call him, and show him to us? For even if he were younger than he is, there could be no impropriety in his talking to us in the presence of you, who are his guardian and cousin.'

'Very well,' he said; 'then I will call him'; and turning to the attendant, he said, 'Call Charmides, and tell him that I want him to come and see a physician about the illness of which he spoke to me the day before yesterday.

Then again addressing me, he added: 'He has been complaining lately of having a headache when he rises in the morning: now why should you not make him believe that you know a cure for the headache?'

'Why not,' I said; 'but will he come?'

'He will be sure to come,' he replied.

He came as he was bidden, and sat down between Critias and me. Great amusement was occasioned by every one pushing with might and main at his neighbour in order to make a place for him next to themselves, until at the two ends of the row one had to get up and the other was rolled over sideways.

Now I, my friend, was beginning to feel awkward; my former bold belief in my powers of conversing with him had vanished. And when Critias told him that I was the person who had the cure, he looked at me in such an indescribable manner, and was just going to ask a question.

And at that moment all the people in the palaestra crowded about us, and, O rare! I caught a sight of the inwards of his garment, and took the flame. Then I could no longer contain myself. I thought how well Cydias understood the nature of love, when, in speaking of a fair youth, he warns someone 'not to bring the fawn in the sight of the lion to be devoured by him,' for I felt that I had been overcome by a sort of wild-beast appetite. But I controlled myself, and when he asked me if I knew the cure of the headache, I answered, but with an effort, that I did know.

'And what is it?' he said.

I replied that it was a kind of leaf, which required to be accompanied by a charm, and if a person would repeat the charm at the same time that he used the cure, he would be made whole; but that without the charm the leaf would be of no avail.

'Then I will write out the charm from your dictation,' he said.

'With my consent?' I said, 'or without my consent?'

'With your consent, Socrates,' he said, laughing.

'Very good,' I said; 'and are you quite sure that you know my name?'

'I ought to know you,' he replied, 'for there is a great deal said about you among my companions; and I remember when I was a child seeing you in company with my cousin Critias.'

'I am glad to find that you remember me,' I said; 'for I shall now be more at home with you and shall be better able to explain the nature of the charm, about which I felt a difficulty before. For the charm will do more, Charmides, than only cure the headache. I dare say that you have heard eminent physicians say to a patient who comes to them with bad eyes, that they cannot cure his eyes by themselves, but that if his eyes are to be cured, his head must be treated; and then again they say that to think of curing the head alone, and not the rest of the body also, is the height of folly. And arguing in this way they apply their methods to the whole body, and try to treat and heal the whole and the part together. Did you ever observe that this is what they say?'

'Yes,' he said.

'And they are right, and you would agree with them?'

'Yes,' he said, 'certainly I should.'

His approving answers reassured me, and I began by degrees to regain confidence, and the vital heat returned.

'Such, Charmides,' I said, 'is the nature of the charm, which I learned when serving with the army from one of the physicians of the Thracian king Zamolxis, who are said to be so skillful that they can even give immortality. This Thracian told me that in these notions of theirs, which I was just now mentioning, the Greek physicians are quite right as far as they go; but Zamolxis, he added, our king, who is also a god, says further, "that as you ought not to attempt to cure the eyes without the head, or the head without the body, so neither ought you to attempt to cure the body without the soul; and this,' he said, 'is the reason why the cure of many diseases is unknown to the physicians of Hellas, because they are ignorant of the whole, which ought to be studied also; for the part can never be well unless the whole is well." For all good and evil, whether in the body or in human nature, originates, as he declared, in the soul, and overflows from thence, as if from the head into the eyes. And therefore if the head and body are to be well, you must begin by curing the soul; that is the first thing. And the cure, my dear youth, has to be effected by the use of certain charms, and these charms are fair words; and by them temperance is implanted in the soul, and where temperance is, there health is speedily imparted, not only to the head, but to the whole body. And he who taught me the cure and the charm at the same time added a special direction: "Let no one," he said, "persuade you to cure the head, until he has first given you his soul to be cured by the charm. For this," he said, "is the great error of our day in the treatment of the human body, that physicians separate the soul from the body." And he added with emphasis, at the same time making me swear to his words, "Let no one, however rich, or noble, or fair, persuade you to give him the cure, without the charm." Now I have sworn, and I must keep my oath, and therefore if you will allow me to apply the Thracian charm first to your soul, as the stranger directed, I will afterwards proceed to apply the cure to your head. But if not, I do not know what I am to do with you, my dear Charmides.'

Critias, when he heard this, said: 'The headache will be an unexpected gain to my young relation, if the pain in his head compels him to improve his mind: and I can tell you, Socrates, that Charmides is not only pre-eminent in beauty among his equals, but also in that quality which is given by the charm; and this, as you say, is temperance?'

'Yes,' I said.

'Then let me tell you that he is the most temperate of human beings, and for his age inferior to none in any quality.'

'Yes,' I said, 'Charmides; and indeed I think that you ought to excel others in all good qualities; for if I am not mistaken there is no one present who could easily point out two Athenian houses, whose union would be likely to produce a better or nobler scion than the two from which you are sprung. There is your father's house, which is descended from Critias the son of Dropidas, whose family has been commemorated in the panegyrical verses of Anacreon, Solon, and many other poets, as famous for beauty and virtue and all other high fortune: and your mother's house is equally distinguished; for your maternal uncle, Pyrilampes, is reputed never to have found his equal, in Persia at the court of the great king, or on the continent of Asia, in all the places to which he went as ambassador, for stature and beauty; that whole family is not a whit inferior to the other. Having such ancestors you ought to be first in all things, and, sweet son of Glaucon, your outward form is no dishonour to any of them. If to beauty you add temperance, and if in other respects you are what Critias declares you to be, then, dear Charmides, blessed art thou, in being the son of thy mother. And here lies the point; for if, as he declares, you have this gift of temperance already, and are temperate enough, in that case you have no need of any charms, whether of Zamolxis or of Abaris the Hyperborean, and I may as well let you have the cure of the head at once; but if you have not yet acquired this quality, I must use the charm before I give you the medicine. Please, therefore, to inform me whether you admit the truth of what Critias has been saying—have you or have you not this quality of temperance?'

Charmides blushed, and the blush heightened his beauty, for modesty is becoming in youth; he then said very ingenuously, that he really could not at once answer, either yes, or no, to the question which I had asked: 'For,' said he, 'if I affirm that I am not temperate, that would be a strange thing for me to say of myself, and also I should give the lie to Critias, and many others who think as he tells you, that I am temperate: but, on the other hand, if I say that I am, I shall have to praise myself, which would be ill manners; and therefore I do not know how to answer you.'

I said to him: 'That is a natural reply, Charmides, and I think that you and I ought together to inquire whether you have this quality about which I am asking or not; and then you will not be compelled to say what you do not like; neither shall I be a rash practitioner of medicine: therefore, if you please, I will share the inquiry with you, but I will not press you if you would rather not.'

'There is nothing which I should like better,' he said; 'and as far as I am concerned you may proceed in the way which you think best.'

'I think,' I said, 'that I had better begin by asking you a question; for if temperance abides in you, you must have an opinion about her; she must give some intimation of her nature and qualities, which may enable you to form a notion of her. Is not that true?'

'Yes,' he said, 'that I think is true.'

'You know your native language,' I said, 'and therefore you must be able to tell what you feel about this.'

'Certainly,' he said.

'In order, then, that I may form a conjecture whether you have temperance abiding in you or not, tell me, I said, what, in your opinion, is Temperance?'

At first he hesitated, and was very unwilling to answer: then he said that he thought temperance was doing things orderly and quietly, such things for example as walking in the streets, and talking, or anything else of that nature. 'In a word,' he said, 'I should answer that, in my opinion, temperance is quietness.'

'Are you right, Charmides?' I said.

'No doubt some would affirm that the quiet are the temperate; but let us see whether these words have any meaning; and first tell me whether you would not acknowledge temperance to be of the class of the noble and good?'

'Yes.'

'But which is best when you are at the writing-master's, to write the same letters quickly or quietly?'

'Quickly.'

'And to read quickly or slowly?'

'Quickly again.'

'And in playing the lyre, or wrestling, quickness or sharpness are far better than quietness and slowness?'

'Yes.'

'And the same holds in boxing and in the pancratium?'

'Certainly.'

'And in leaping and running and in bodily exercises generally, quickness and agility are good; slowness, and inactivity, and quietness, are bad?'

'That is evident.'

'Then,' I said, 'in all bodily actions, not quietness, but the greatest agility and quickness, is noblest and best?'

'Yes, certainly.'

'And is temperance a good?'

'Yes.'

'Then, in reference to the body, not quietness, but quickness will be the higher degree of temperance, if temperance is a good?'

'True,' he said.

'And which, I said, is better—facility in learning, or difficulty in learning?'

'Facility.'

'Yes,' I said; 'and facility in learning is learning quickly, and difficulty in learning is learning quietly and slowly?'

'True.'

'And is it not better to teach another quickly and energetically, rather than quietly and slowly?'

'Yes.'

'And which is better, to call to mind, and to remember, quickly and readily, or quietly and slowly?'

'The former.'

'And is not shrewdness a quickness or cleverness of the soul, and not a quietness?'

'True.'

'And is it not best to understand what is said, whether at the writing-master's or the music-master's, or anywhere else, not as quietly as possible, but as quickly as possible?'

'Yes.'

'And in the searchings or deliberations of the soul, not the quietest, as I imagine, and he who with difficulty deliberates and discovers, is thought worthy of praise, but he who does so most easily and quickly?'

'Quite true,' he said.

'And in all that concerns either body or soul, swiftness and activity are clearly better than slowness and quietness?'

'Clearly they are.'

'Then temperance is not quietness, nor is the temperate life quiet, certainly not upon this view; for the life which is temperate is supposed to be the good. And of two things, one is true,—either never, or very seldom, do the quiet actions in life appear to be better than the quick and energetic ones; or supposing that of the nobler actions, there are as many quiet, as quick and vehement: still, even if we grant this, temperance will not be acting quietly any more than acting quickly and energetically, either in walking or talking or in anything else; nor will the quiet life be more temperate than the unquiet, seeing that temperance is admitted by us to be a good and noble thing, and the quick have been shown to be as good as the quiet.'

'I think,' he said, 'Socrates, that you are right.'

'Then once more, Charmides,' I said, 'fix your attention, and look within; consider the effect which temperance has upon yourself, and

CHARMIDES

the nature of that which has the effect. Think over all this, and, like a brave youth, tell me—What is temperance?'

After a moment's pause, in which he made a real manly effort to think, he said: 'My opinion is, Socrates, that temperance makes a man ashamed or modest, and that temperance is the same as modesty.'

'Very good,' I said; 'and did you not admit, just now, that temperance is noble?'

'Yes, certainly,' he said.

'And the temperate are also good?'

'Yes.'

'And can that be good which does not make men good?'

'Certainly not.'

'And you would infer that temperance is not only noble, but also good?'

'That is my opinion.'

'Well,' I said; 'but surely you would agree with Homer when he says, "Modesty is not good for a needy man"?'

'Yes,' he said; 'I agree.'

'Then I suppose that modesty is and is not good?'

'Clearly.'

'But temperance, whose presence makes men only good, and not bad, is always good? That appears to me to be as you say. And the inference is that temperance cannot be modesty—if temperance is a good, and if modesty is as much an evil as a good?'

'All that, Socrates, appears to me to be true; but I should like to know what you think about another definition of temperance, which I just now remember to have heard from someone, who said, "That temperance is doing our own business." Was he right who affirmed that?'

'You monster!' I said; 'this is what Critias, or some philosopher has told you.'

'Someone else, then,' said Critias; 'for certainly I have not.'

'But what matter,' said Charmides, 'from whom I heard this?'

'No matter at all,' I replied; 'for the point is not who said the words, but whether they are true or not.'

'There you are in the right, Socrates,' he replied.

'To be sure,' I said; 'yet I doubt whether we shall ever be able to discover their truth or falsehood; for they are a kind of riddle.'

'What makes you think so?' he said.

'Because,' I said, 'he who uttered them seems to me to have meant one thing, and said another. Is the scribe, for example, to be regarded as doing nothing when he reads or writes? I should rather think that he was doing something. And does the scribe write or read, or teach you boys to write or read, your own names only, or did you write your enemies' names as well as your own and your friends'?'

'As much one as the other.'

'And was there anything meddling or intemperate in this?'

'Certainly not.'

'And yet if reading and writing are the same as doing, you were doing what was not your own business?'

'But they are the same as doing.'

'And the healing art, my friend, and building, and weaving, and doing anything whatever which is done by art—these all clearly come under the head of doing?'

'Certainly.'

'And do you think that a state would be well ordered by a law which compelled every man to weave and wash his own coat, and make his own shoes, and his own flask and strigil, and other implements, on this principle of everyone doing and performing his own, and abstaining from what is not his own?'

'I think not,' he said.

'But,' I said, 'a temperate state will be a well-ordered state.'

'Of course,' he replied.

'Then temperance,' I said, 'will not be doing one's own business; not at least in this way, or doing things of this sort?'

'Clearly not.'

'Then, as I was just now saying, he who declared that temperance is a man doing his own business had another and a hidden meaning; for I do not think that he could have been such a fool as to mean this. Was he a fool who told you, Charmides?'

'Nay,' he replied, 'I certainly thought him a very wise man.'

'Then I am quite certain that he put forth his definition as a riddle, thinking that no one would know the meaning of the words "doing his own business."'

'I dare say,' he replied. 'And what is the meaning of a man doing his own business? Can you tell me?'

'Indeed, I cannot; and I should not wonder if the man himself who used this phrase did not understand what he was saying.'

Whereupon he laughed slyly, and looked at Critias.

Critias had long been showing uneasiness, for he felt that he had a reputation to maintain with Charmides and the rest of the company.

He had, however, hitherto managed to restrain himself; but now he could no longer forbear, and I am convinced of the truth of the suspicion which I entertained at the time, that Charmides had heard this answer about temperance from Critias.

And Charmides, who did not want to answer himself, but to make Critias answer, tried to stir him up.

He went on pointing out that he had been refuted, at which Critias grew angry, and appeared, as I thought, inclined to quarrel with him; just as a poet might quarrel with an actor who spoiled his poems in repeating them; so he looked hard at him and said—'Do you imagine, Charmides, that the author of this definition of temperance did not understand the meaning of his own words, because you do not understand them?'

'Why, at his age,' I said, 'most excellent Critias, he can hardly be expected to understand; but you, who are older, and have studied, may well be assumed to know the meaning of them; and therefore, if you agree with him, and accept his definition of temperance, I would much rather argue with you than with him about the truth or falsehood of the definition.'

'I entirely agree,' said Critias, 'and accept the definition.'

'Very good,' I said; 'and now let me repeat my question—Do you admit, as I was just now saying, that all craftsmen make or do something?'

'I do.'

'And do they make or do their own business only, or that of others also?'

'They make or do that of others also.'

'And are they temperate, seeing that they make not for themselves or their own business only?'

'Why not?' he said.

'No objection on my part,' I said, 'but there may be a difficulty on his who proposes as a definition of temperance, "doing one's own business," and then says that there is no reason why those who do the business of others should not be temperate.'

'Nay†,' said he; 'did I ever acknowledge that those who do the business of others are temperate? I said, those who make, not those who do.'

'What!' I asked; 'do you mean to say that doing and making are not the same?'

'No more,' he replied, 'than making or working are the same; thus much I have learned from Hesiod, who says that "work is no disgrace." Now do you imagine that if he had meant by working and doing such things as you were describing, he would have said that

---

†The English reader has to observe that the word 'make' (Greek), in Greek, has also the sense of 'do' (Greek).

there was no disgrace in them—for example, in the manufacture of shoes, or in selling pickles, or sitting for hire in a house of ill-fame? That, Socrates, is not to be supposed: but I conceive him to have distinguished making from doing and work; and, while admitting that the making anything might sometimes become a disgrace, when the employment was not honourable, to have thought that work was never any disgrace at all. For things nobly and usefully made he called works; and such makings he called workings, and doings; and he must be supposed to have called such things only man's proper business, and what is hurtful, not his business: and in that sense Hesiod, and any other wise man, may be reasonably supposed to call him wise who does his own work.'

'O Critias,' I said, 'no sooner had you opened your mouth, than I pretty well knew that you would call that which is proper to a man, and that which is his own, good; and that the makings of the good you would call doings, for I am no stranger to the endless distinctions which Prodicus draws about names. Now I have no objection to your giving names any signification which you please, if you will only tell me what you mean by them. Please then to begin again, and be a little plainer. Do you mean that this doing or making, or whatever is the word which you would use, of good actions, is temperance?'

'I do,' he said.

'Then not he who does evil, but he who does good, is temperate?'

'Yes,' he said; 'and you, friend, would agree.'

'No matter whether I should or not; just now, not what I think, but what you are saying, is the point at issue.'

'Well,' he answered; 'I mean to say, that he who does evil, and not good, is not temperate; and that he is temperate who does good, and not evil: for temperance I define in plain words to be the doing of good actions.'

'And you may be very likely right in what you are saying; but I am curious to know whether you imagine that temperate men are ignorant of their own temperance?'

'I do not think so,' he said.

'And yet were you not saying, just now, that craftsmen might be temperate in doing another's work, as well as in doing their own?'

'I was,' he replied; 'but what is your drift?'

'I have no particular drift, but I wish that you would tell me whether a physician who cures a patient may do good to himself and good to another also?'

'I think that he may.'

'And he who does so does his duty?'

'Yes.'

'And does not he who does his duty act temperately or wisely?'

'Yes, he acts wisely.'

'But must the physician necessarily know when his treatment is likely to prove beneficial, and when not? Or must the craftsman necessarily know when he is likely to be benefited, and when not to be benefited, by the work which he is doing?'

'I suppose not.'

'Then, I said, he may sometimes do good or harm, and not know what he is himself doing, and yet, in doing good, as you say, he has done temperately or wisely. Was not that your statement?'

'Yes.'

'Then, as would seem, in doing good, he may act wisely or temperately, and be wise or temperate, but not know his own wisdom or temperance?'

'But that, Socrates,' he said, 'is impossible; and therefore if this is, as you imply, the necessary consequence of any of my previous admissions, I will withdraw them, rather than admit that a man can be temperate or wise who does not know himself; and I am not ashamed to confess that I was in error. For self-knowledge would certainly be maintained by me to be the very essence of knowledge, and in this I agree with him who dedicated the inscription, "Know thyself!" at Delphi. That word, if I am not mistaken, is put there as a sort of salutation which the god addresses to those who enter the temple; as much as to say that the ordinary salutation of "Hail!" is not right, and that the exhortation "Be temperate!" would be a far better way of saluting one another. The notion of him who dedicated the inscription was, as I believe, that the god speaks to those who enter his temple, not as men speak; but, when a worshipper enters, the first word which he hears is "Be temperate!" This, however, like a prophet he expresses in a sort of riddle, for "Know thyself!" and "Be temperate!" are the same, as I maintain, and as the letters imply, and yet they may be easily misunderstood; and succeeding sages who added "Never too much," or, "Give a pledge, and evil is nigh at hand," would appear to have so misunderstood them; for they imagined that "Know thyself!" was a piece of advice which the god gave, and not his salutation of the worshippers at their first coming in; and they dedicated their own inscription under the idea that they too would give equally useful pieces of advice. Shall I tell you, Socrates, why I say all this? My object is to leave the previous discussion (in which I know not whether you or I are more right, but, at any rate, no clear result was attained), and to raise a new one in which I will attempt to prove, if you deny, that temperance is self-knowledge.'

'Yes,' I said, 'Critias; but you come to me as though I professed to know about the questions which I ask, and as though I could, if I only would, agree with you. Whereas the fact is that I inquire with you into the truth of that which is advanced from time to time, just because I do not know; and when I have inquired, I will say whether I agree with you or not. Please then to allow me time to reflect.'

'Reflect,' he said.

'I am reflecting,' I replied, 'and discover that temperance, or wisdom, if implying a knowledge of anything, must be a science, and a science of something.'

'Yes,' he said; 'the science of itself.'

'Is not medicine,' I said, 'the science of health?'

'True.'

'And suppose,' I said, 'that I were asked by you what is the use or effect of medicine, which is this science of health, I should answer that medicine is of very great use in producing health, which, as you will admit, is an excellent effect.'

'Granted.'

'And if you were to ask me, what is the result or effect of architecture, which is the science of building, I should say houses, and so of other arts, which all have their different results. Now I want you, Critias, to answer a similar question about temperance, or wisdom, which, according to you, is the science of itself. Admitting this view, I ask of you, what good work, worthy of the name wise, does temperance or wisdom, which is the science of itself, effect? Answer me.'

'That is not the true way of pursuing the inquiry, Socrates,' he said; 'for wisdom is not like the other sciences, any more than they are like one another: but you proceed as if they were alike. For tell me,' he said, 'what result is there of computation or geometry, in the same sense as a house is the result of building, or a garment of weaving, or any other work of any other art? Can you show me any such result of them? You cannot.'

'That is true,' I said; 'but still each of these sciences has a subject which is different from the science. I can show you that the art of computation has to do with odd and even numbers in their numerical relations to themselves and to each other. Is not that true?'

'Yes,' he said.

'And the odd and even numbers are not the same with the art of computation?'

'They are not.'

'The art of weighing, again, has to do with lighter and heavier; but the art of weighing is one thing, and the heavy and the light another. Do you admit that?'

'Yes.'

'Now, I want to know, what is that which is not wisdom, and of which wisdom is the science?'

'You are just falling into the old error, Socrates,' he said. 'You come asking in what wisdom or temperance differs from the other sciences, and then you try to discover some respect in which they are alike; but they are not, for all the other sciences are of something else, and not of themselves; wisdom alone is a science of other sciences, and of itself. And of this, as I believe, you are very well aware: and that you are only doing what you denied that you were doing just now, trying to refute me, instead of pursuing the argument.'

'And what if I am? How can you think that I have any other motive in refuting you but what I should have in examining into myself? Which motive would be just a fear of my unconsciously fancying that I knew something of which I was ignorant. And at this moment I pursue the argument chiefly for my own sake, and perhaps in some degree also for the sake of my other friends. For is not the discovery of things as they truly are, a good common to all mankind?'

'Yes, certainly, Socrates,' he said.

'Then,' I said, 'be cheerful, sweet sir, and give your opinion in answer to the question which I asked, never minding whether Critias or Socrates is the person refuted; attend only to the argument, and see what will come of the refutation.'

'I think that you are right,' he replied; 'and I will do as you say.'

'Tell me, then,' I said, 'what you mean to affirm about wisdom.'

'I mean to say that wisdom is the only science which is the science of itself as well as of the other sciences.'

'But the science of science,' I said, 'will also be the science of the absence of science.'

'Very true,' he said.

'Then the wise or temperate man, and he only, will know himself, and be able to examine what he knows or does not know, and to see what others know and think that they know and do really know; and what they do not know, and fancy that they know, when they do not. No other person will be able to do this. And this is wisdom and temperance and self-knowledge—for a man to know what he knows, and what he does not know. That is your meaning?'

'Yes,' he said.

'Now then,' I said, 'making an offering of the third or last argument to Zeus the Saviour, let us begin again, and ask, in the first place, whether it is or is not possible for a person to know that he knows and does not know what he knows and does not know; and in the second place, whether, if perfectly possible, such knowledge is of any use.'

'That is what we have to consider,' he said.

'And here, Critias,' I said, 'I hope that you will find a way out of a difficulty into which I have got myself. Shall I tell you the nature of the difficulty?'

'By all means,' he replied.

'Does not what you have been saying, if true, amount to this: that there must be a single science which is wholly a science of itself and of other sciences, and that the same is also the science of the absence of science?'

'Yes.'

'But consider how monstrous this proposition is, my friend: in any parallel case, the impossibility will be transparent to you.'

'How is that? And in what cases do you mean?'

'In such cases as this: Suppose that there is a kind of vision which is not like ordinary vision, but a vision of itself and of other sorts of vision, and of the defect of them, which in seeing sees no color, but only itself and other sorts of vision: Do you think that there is such a kind of vision?'

'Certainly not.'

'Or is there a kind of hearing which hears no sound at all, but only itself and other sorts of hearing, or the defects of them?'

'There is not.'

'Or take all the senses: can you imagine that there is any sense of itself and of other senses, but which is incapable of perceiving the objects of the senses?'

'I think not.'

'Could there be any desire which is not the desire of any pleasure, but of itself, and of all other desires?'

'Certainly not.'

'Or can you imagine a wish which wishes for no good, but only for itself and all other wishes?'

'I should answer, no.'

'Or would you say that there is a love which is not the love of beauty, but of itself and of other loves?'

'I should not.'

'Or did you ever know of a fear which fears itself or other fears, but has no object of fear?'

'I never did,' he said.

'Or of an opinion which is an opinion of itself and of other opinions, and which has no opinion on the subjects of opinion in general?'

'Certainly not.'

'But surely we are assuming a science of this kind, which, having no subject-matter, is a science of itself and of the other sciences?'

'Yes, that is what is affirmed.'

'But how strange is this, if it be indeed true: we must not however as yet absolutely deny the possibility of such a science; let us rather consider the matter.'

'You are quite right.'

'Well then, this science of which we are speaking is a science of something, and is of a nature to be a science of something?'

'Yes.'

'Just as that which is greater is of a nature to be greater than something else?'[†]

'Yes.'

'Which is less, if the other is conceived to be greater?'

'To be sure.'

'And if we could find something which is at once greater than itself, and greater than other great things, but not greater than those things in comparison of which the others are greater, then that thing would have the property of being greater and also less than itself?'

'That, Socrates,' he said, 'is the inevitable inference.'

[†]Socrates is intending to show that science differs from the object of science, as any other relative differs from the object of relation.

But where there is comparison—greater, less, heavier, lighter, and the like—a relation to self as well as to other things involves an absolute contradiction; and in other cases, as in the case of the senses, is hardly conceivable.

The use of the genitive after the comparative in Greek, (Greek), creates an unavoidable obscurity in the translation.

'Or if there be a double which is double of itself and of other doubles, these will be halves; for the double is relative to the half?'

'That is true.'

'And that which is greater than itself will also be less, and that which is heavier will also be lighter, and that which is older will also be younger: and the same of other things; that which has a nature relative to self will retain also the nature of its object: I mean to say, for example, that hearing is, as we say, of sound or voice. Is that true?'

'Yes.'

'Then if hearing hears itself, it must hear a voice; for there is no other way of hearing.'

'Certainly.'

'And sight also, my excellent friend, if it sees itself must see a color, for sight cannot see that which has no color.'

'No.'

'Do you remark, Critias, that in several of the examples which have been recited the notion of a relation to self is altogether inadmissible, and in other cases hardly credible—inadmissible, for example, in the case of magnitudes, numbers, and the like?'

'Very true.'

'But in the case of hearing and sight, or in the power of self-motion, and the power of heat to burn, this relation to self will be regarded as incredible by some, but perhaps not by others. And some great man, my friend, is wanted, who will satisfactorily determine for us, whether there is nothing which has an inherent property of relation to self, or some things only and not others; and whether in this class of self-related things, if there be such a class, that science which is called wisdom or temperance is included. I altogether distrust my own power of determining these matters: I am not certain whether there is such a science of science at all; and even if there be, I should not acknowledge this to be wisdom or temperance, until I can also see whether such a science would or would not do us any good; for I have an impression that temperance is a benefit and a good. And therefore, O son of Callaeschrus, as you maintain that temperance or wisdom is a science of science, and also of the absence of science, I will request you to show in the first place, as I was saying before, the possibility, and in the second place, the advantage, of such a science; and then perhaps you may satisfy me that you are right in your view of temperance.'

Critias heard me say this, and saw that I was in a difficulty; and as one person when another yawns in his presence catches the infection of yawning from him, so did he seem to be driven into a difficulty by my difficulty. But as he had a reputation to maintain, he was ashamed to admit before the company that he could not answer my challenge or determine the question at issue; and he made an unintelligible attempt to hide his perplexity.

In order that the argument might proceed, I said to him, 'Well then Critias, if you like, let us assume that there is this science of science; whether the assumption is right or wrong may hereafter be investigated. Admitting the existence of it, will you tell me how such a science enables us to distinguish what we know or do not know, which, as we were saying, is self-knowledge or wisdom: so we were saying?'

'Yes, Socrates,' he said; 'and that I think is certainly true: for he who has this science or knowledge which knows itself will become like the knowledge which he has, in the same way that he who has swiftness will be swift, and he who has beauty will be beautiful, and he who has knowledge will know. In the same way he who has that knowledge which is self-knowing, will know himself.'

'I do not doubt,' I said, 'that a man will know himself, when he possesses that which has self-knowledge: but what necessity is there that, having this, he should know what he knows and what he does not know?'

'Because, Socrates, they are the same.'

'Very likely,' I said; 'but I remain as stupid as ever; for still I fail to comprehend how this knowing what you know and do not know is the same as the knowledge of self.'

'What do you mean?' he said.

'This is what I mean,' I replied: 'I will admit that there is a science of science—can this do more than determine that of two things one is and the other is not science or knowledge?'

'No, just that.'

'But is knowledge or want of knowledge of health the same as knowledge or want of knowledge of justice?'

'Certainly not.'

'The one is medicine, and the other is politics; whereas that of which we are speaking is knowledge pure and simple.'

'Very true.'

'And if a man knows only, and has only knowledge of knowledge, and has no further knowledge of health and justice, the probability is that he will only know that he knows something, and has a certain knowledge, whether concerning himself or other men.'

'True.'

'Then how will this knowledge or science teach him to know what he knows? Say that he knows health—not wisdom or temperance, but the art of medicine has taught it to him;—and he has learned harmony from the art of music, and building from the art of building—neither, from wisdom or temperance: and the same of other things.'

'That is evident.'

'How will wisdom, regarded only as a knowledge of knowledge or science of science, ever teach him that he knows health, or that he knows building?'

'It is impossible.'

'Then he who is ignorant of these things will only know that he knows, but not what he knows?'

'True.'

'Then wisdom or being wise appears to be not the knowledge of the things which we do or do not know, but only the knowledge that we know or do not know?'

'That is the inference.'

'Then he who has this knowledge will not be able to examine whether a pretender knows or does not know that which he says that he knows: he will only know that he has a knowledge of some kind; but wisdom will not show him of what the knowledge is?'

'Plainly not.'

'Neither will he be able to distinguish the pretender in medicine from the true physician, nor between any other true and false professor of knowledge. Let us consider the matter in this way: If the wise man or any other man wants to distinguish the true physician from the false, how will he proceed? He will not talk to him about medicine; and that, as we were saying, is the only thing which the physician understands.'

'True.'

'And, on the other hand, the physician knows nothing of science, for this has been assumed to be the province of wisdom.'

'True.'

'And further, since medicine is science, we must infer that he does not know anything of medicine.'

'Exactly.'

'Then the wise man may indeed know that the physician has some kind of science or knowledge; but when he wants to discover the nature of this he will ask, what is the subject-matter? For the several sciences are distinguished not by the mere fact that they are sciences, but by the nature of their subjects. Is not that true?'

'Quite true.'

'And medicine is distinguished from other sciences as having the subject-matter of health and disease?'

'Yes.'

'And he who would inquire into the nature of medicine must pursue the inquiry into health and disease, and not into what is extraneous?'

'True.'

'And he who judges rightly will judge of the physician as a physician in what relates to these?'

'He will.'

'He will consider whether what he says is true, and whether what he does is right, in relation to health and disease?'

'He will.'

'But can anyone attain the knowledge of either unless he have a knowledge of medicine?'

'He cannot.'

'No one at all, it would seem, except the physician can have this knowledge; and therefore not the wise man; he would have to be a physician as well as a wise man.'

'Very true.'

'Then, assuredly, wisdom or temperance, if only a science of science, and of the absence of science or knowledge, will not be able to distinguish the physician who knows from one who does not know but pretends or thinks that he knows, or any other professor of anything at all; like any other artist, he will only know his fellow in art or wisdom, and no one else.'

'That is evident,' he said.

'But then what profit, Critias,' I said, 'is there any longer in wisdom or temperance which yet remains, if this is wisdom? If, indeed, as we were supposing at first, the wise man had been able to distinguish what he knew and did not know, and that he knew the one and did not know the other, and to recognize a similar faculty of discernment in others, there would certainly have been a great advantage in being wise; for then we should never have made a mistake, but have passed through life the unerring guides of ourselves and of those who are under us; and we should not have attempted to do what we did not know, but we should have found out those who knew, and have handed the business over to them and trusted in them; nor should we have allowed those who were under us to do anything which they were not likely to do well; and they would be likely to do well just that of which they had knowledge; and the house or state which was ordered or administered under the guidance of wisdom, and everything else of which wisdom was the lord, would have been well ordered; for truth guiding, and error having been eliminated, in all their doings, men would have done well, and would have been happy. Was not this, Critias, what we spoke of as the great advantage of wisdom—to know what is known and what is unknown to us?'

'Very true,' he said.

'And now you perceive,' I said, 'that no such science is to be found anywhere.'

'I perceive,' he said.

'May we assume then,' I said, 'that wisdom, viewed in this new light merely as a knowledge of knowledge and ignorance, has this advantage: that he who possesses such knowledge will more easily learn anything which he learns; and that everything will be clearer to him, because, in addition to the knowledge of individuals, he sees the science, and this also will better enable him to test the knowledge which others have of what he knows himself; whereas the inquirer who is without this knowledge may be supposed to have a feebler and weaker insight? Are not these, my friend, the real advantages which are to be gained from wisdom? And are not we looking and seeking after something more than is to be found in her?'

'That is very likely,' he said.

'That is very likely,' I said; 'and very likely, too, we have been inquiring to no purpose; as I am led to infer, because I observe that if this is wisdom, some strange consequences would follow. Let us, if you please, assume the possibility of this science of sciences, and further admit and allow, as was originally suggested, that wisdom is the knowledge of what we know and do not know. Assuming all this, still, upon further consideration, I am doubtful, Critias, whether wisdom, such as this, would do us much good. For we were wrong, I think, in supposing, as we were saying just now, that such wisdom ordering the government of house or state would be a great benefit.'

'How so?' he said.

'Why,' I said, 'we were far too ready to admit the great benefits which mankind would obtain from their severally doing the things which they knew, and committing the things of which they are ignorant to those who were better acquainted with them. Were we not right in making that admission? I think not.'

'How very strange, Socrates!'

'By the dog of Egypt,' I said, 'there I agree with you; and I was thinking as much just now when I said that strange consequences would follow, and that I was afraid we were on the wrong track; for however ready we may be to admit that this is wisdom, I certainly cannot make out what good this sort of thing does to us.'

'What do you mean?' he said; 'I wish that you could make me understand what you mean.'

'I dare say that what I am saying is nonsense,' I replied; 'and yet if a man has any feeling of what is due to himself, he cannot let the thought which comes into his mind pass away unheeded and unexamined.'

'I like that,' he said.

'Hear, then,' I said, 'my own dream; whether coming through the horn or the ivory gate, I cannot tell. The dream is this: Let us suppose that wisdom is such as we are now defining, and that she has absolute sway over us; then each action will be done according to the arts or sciences, and no one professing to be a pilot when he is not, or any physician or general, or any one else pretending to know matters of which he is ignorant, will deceive or elude us; our health will be improved; our safety at sea, and also in battle, will be assured; our coats and shoes, and all other instruments and implements will be skillfully made, because the workmen will be good and true. Aye, and if you please, you may suppose that prophecy, which is the knowledge of the future, will be under the control of wisdom, and that she will deter deceivers and set up the true prophets in their place as the revealers of the future. Now I quite agree that mankind, thus provided, would live and act according to knowledge, for wisdom would watch and prevent ignorance from intruding on us. But whether by acting according to knowledge we shall act well and be happy, my dear Critias— this is a point which we have not yet been able to determine.'

'Yet I think,' he replied, 'that if you discard knowledge, you will hardly find the crown of happiness in anything else.'

'But of what is this knowledge?' I said. 'Just answer me that small question. Do you mean a knowledge of shoemaking?'

'God forbid.'

'Or of working in brass?'

'Certainly not.'

'Or in wool, or wood, or anything of that sort?'

'No, I do not.'

'Then,' I said, 'we are giving up the doctrine that he who lives according to knowledge is happy, for these live according to knowledge, and yet they are not allowed by you to be happy; but I think that you mean to confine happiness to particular individuals who live according to knowledge, such for example as the prophet, who, as I was saying, knows the future. Is it of him you are speaking or of someone else?'

'Yes, I mean him, but there are others as well.'

'Yes,' I said, 'someone who knows the past and present as well as the future, and is ignorant of nothing. Let us suppose that there is such a person, and if there is, you will allow that he is the most knowing of all living men.'

'Certainly he is.'

'Yet I should like to know one thing more: which of the different kinds of knowledge makes him happy? Or do all equally make him happy?'

'Not all equally,' he replied.

'But which most tends to make him happy? The knowledge of what past, present, or future thing? May I infer this to be the knowledge of the game of draughts?'

'Nonsense about the game of draughts.'

'Or of computation?'

'No.'

'Or of health?'

'That is nearer the truth,' he said.

'And that knowledge which is nearest of all,' I said, 'is the knowledge of what?'

'The knowledge with which he discerns good and evil.'

'Monster!' I said; 'you have been carrying me round in a circle, and all this time hiding from me the fact that the life according to knowledge is not that which makes men act rightly and be happy, not even if knowledge include all the sciences, but one science only, that of good and evil. For, let me ask you, Critias, whether, if you take away this, medicine will not equally give health, and shoemaking equally produce shoes, and the art of the weaver clothes?—whether the art of the pilot will not equally save our lives at sea, and the art of the general in war?'

'Quite so.'

'And yet, my dear Critias, none of these things will be well or beneficially done, if the science of the good be wanting.'

'True.'

'But that science is not wisdom or temperance, but a science of human advantage; not a science of other sciences, or of ignorance, but of good and evil: and if this be of use, then wisdom or temperance will not be of use.'

'And why,' he replied, 'will not wisdom be of use? For, however much we assume that wisdom is a science of sciences, and has a sway over other sciences, surely she will have this particular science of the good under her control, and in this way will benefit us.'

'And will wisdom give health?' I said; 'is not this rather the effect of medicine? Or does wisdom do the work of any of the other arts— do they not each of them do their own work? Have we not long ago asseverated that wisdom is only the knowledge of knowledge and of ignorance, and of nothing else?'

'That is obvious.'

'Then wisdom will not be the producer of health.'

'Certainly not.'

'The art of health is different.'

'Yes, different.'

'Nor does wisdom give advantage, my good friend; for that again we have just now been attributing to another art.'

'Very true.'

'How then can wisdom be advantageous, when giving no advantage?'

'That, Socrates, is certainly inconceivable.'

'You see then, Critias, that I was not far wrong in fearing that I could have no sound notion about wisdom; I was quite right in depreciating myself; for that which is admitted to be the best of all things would never have seemed to us useless, if I had been good for anything at an inquiry. But now I have been utterly defeated, and have failed to discover what that is to which the imposer of names gave this name of temperance or wisdom. And yet many more admissions were made by us than could be fairly granted; for we admitted that there was a science of science, although the argument said No, and protested against us; and we admitted further, that this science knew the works of the other sciences (although this too was denied by the argument), because we wanted to show that the wise man had knowledge of what he knew and did not know; also we nobly disregarded, and never even considered, the impossibility of a man knowing in a sort of way that which he does not know at all; for our assumption was, that he knows that which he does not know; than which nothing, as I think, can be more irrational. And yet, after finding us so easy and good-natured, the inquiry is still unable to discover the truth; but mocks us to a degree, and has gone out of its way to prove the inutility of that which we admitted only by a sort of supposition and fiction to be the true definition of temperance or wisdom: which result, as far as I am concerned, is not so much to be lamented,' I said. 'But for your sake, Charmides, I am very sorry— that you, having such beauty and such wisdom and temperance of soul, should have no profit or good in life from your wisdom and temperance. And still more am I grieved about the charm which I learned with so much pain, and to so little profit, from the Thracian, for the sake of a thing which is nothing worth. I think indeed that there is a mistake, and that I must be a bad inquirer, for wisdom or temperance I believe to be really a great good; and happy are you, Charmides, if you certainly possess it. Wherefore examine yourself, and see whether you have this gift and can do without the charm; for if you can, I would rather advise you to regard me simply as a fool who is never able to reason out anything; and to rest assured that the more wise and temperate you are, the happier you will be.'

Charmides said: 'I am sure that I do not know, Socrates, whether I have or have not this gift of wisdom and temperance; for how can I know whether I have a thing, of which even you and Critias are, as you say, unable to discover the nature?—not that I believe you. And further, I am sure, Socrates, that I do need the charm, and as far as I am concerned, I shall be willing to be charmed by you daily, until you say that I have had enough.'

'Very good, Charmides,' said Critias; 'if you do this I shall have a proof of your temperance, that is, if you allow yourself to be charmed by Socrates, and never desert him at all.'

'You may depend on my following and not deserting him,' said Charmides: 'if you who are my guardian command me, I should be very wrong not to obey you.'

'And I do command you,' he said.

'Then I will do as you say, and begin this very day.'

'You sirs,' I said, 'what are you conspiring about?'

'We are not conspiring,' said Charmides, 'we have conspired already.'

'And are you about to use violence, without even going through the forms of justice?'

'Yes, I shall use violence,' he replied, 'since he orders me; and therefore you had better consider well.'

'But the time for consideration has passed,' I said, 'when violence is employed; and you, when you are determined on anything, and in the mood of violence, are irresistible.'

'Do not you resist me then,' he said.

'I will not resist you,' I replied.

Preview of Morris B. Kaplan's Introduction to Xenophon's

MEMORABLE THOUGHTS OF SOCRATES

Who was Socrates? What did he think and teach? Why should we remember him? These questions are not so easy to answer as they may appear. Of course, Socrates was a founding figure of Western philosophy, the teacher of Plato, and major influence on Aristotle. The Roman orator and politician Cicero said that Socrates brought philosophy down from the heavens and established it in households and the marketplace. Not only that, but to this day he lends his name to the "Socratic method" by which law professors introduce students to the analysis and application of general rules and concepts.

What complicates the questions above is the fact that Socrates left no writing of his own to convey his "memorable thoughts." We know that Socrates lived in Athens, fought in its army during the war against Sparta, and was tried by jury for "impiety" and "corrupting the youth". Convicted and condemned to death, he rejected an offer to escape arranged by his friends and was executed in 399 BCE at the age of seventy. To put flesh on these bare bones of historical fact, we must rely on accounts of his life and thought left by his students and friends.

In "The Clouds," first produced in 423 BCE, the comic playwright Aristophanes portrayed Socrates as the proprietor of the "thinkery" where he offered, for a fee, to teach students legal argumentation and natural science. Caricatured as a combination shyster lawyer and crackpot scientist, Socrates stands in for the sophists and natural philosophers who contributed to Athenian intellectual life during what one scholar has called "the fifth century enlightenment." In his account of Socrates' defense speech, "Apology," Plato mentions the play as a source of prejudice against his teacher. To redress the balance, Plato wrote dramatic dialogues in which Socrates engages his fellow citizens in examining concepts such as piety, courage, self-control and friendship. Plato's Socrates asks his interlocutors to define what these things mean to them and then questions them to test the consistency and coherence of their ideas.

Most frequently, these conversations end inconclusively, with the discovery of *aporia* or difficulties that require further thought. In "Apology" Plato wrote Socrates as insisting that, whereas others in the city loudly proclaim expertise they cannot justify, his only claim to wisdom consists in knowing that he knows nothing. In dialogues written decades later, Plato appears to use Socrates to expound his own ethical and metaphysical speculations. (In founding the Academy in Athens, Plato established one of the first institutions of higher education where people from all over the world came to study. Among them was Aristotle, whose treatises made him "the Master of those who know" for centuries.)

Xenophon offers a rather different picture in *Memorable Thoughts of Socrates*. Like Plato, he was a contemporary who was much influenced by his friendship with the older Socrates. However, he was a very different kind of man. Whereas young Plato was torn between political ambition and artistic aspiration, Xenophon combined the management of his landed estates with a career as a soldier. Exiled from Athens a couple years before Socrates' trial, he fought for Cyrus in his campaign to become ruler of Persia, as a mercenary in Thrace, and eventually for Sparta. He prospered there for many years before returning to Athens where he died around 354 BCE. Xenophon is best known for his historical writings, including accounts of the end of the Peloponnesian War and of his own ill-fated Persian expedition. However, his Socratic writings also endured and influenced the interpretations of major nineteenth century thinkers like Hegel, Kierkegaard and Nietzsche.

In addition to *Memorable Thoughts of Socrates*, this volume includes two important shorter pieces, Xenophon's versions of "The Apology" and "The Symposium, or the Banquet". ("The Estate-Manager", a treatise in which Socrates also figures, is not included here.) Scholars have debated for centuries whether Xenophon or Plato offers a more accurate picture of the historical Socrates. Perhaps the best we can do is to imagine someone with the intellectual power to inspire the speculative Plato and enough good sense to impress the more worldly Xenophon. Ultimately the reader is left to her own devices, but these texts offer an intriguing counterpoint to the more orthodox Platonic portrait. The committed student might undertake a detailed comparison between Plato's "Socratic Dialogues" and Xenophon's depictions. However, even the more casual reader may enjoy the vivid portrait drawn here.

Xenophon's Socrates is certainly a down-to-earth figure, although sometimes he seems even weirder than the Platonic philosopher. In his version of "The Apology," Xenophon presents a conversation between Socrates and a friend in which the accused man explains why he has not bothered to prepare his defense. At the age of seventy, Socrates knows he will die soon in any event; he can expect a future of declining power and increasing discomfort. By executing him, the Athenians will offer an easy exit! (Drinking hemlock was believed to produce a painless and gentle death.) Besides, Socrates' divine sign had prohibited him from pandering to his jury with insincere apologies and emotional appeals for mercy. Xenophon repeatedly emphasizes Socrates' religious orthodoxy.

He has always participated in the city's rituals and sacrifices; his "daimon" is another oracle through which the gods offer their guidance. Socrates cannot possibly "corrupt the youth" since his teaching is designed to promote virtue and respect for both human and divine law.

Defending Socrates against the charges of which he was convicted is the central aim of Xenophon's *Memorable Thoughts of Socrates*. (So many Athenians came to regret the philosopher's execution that writers often wrote their own defenses in the decades after his death. The Socratic "Apology" became a genre in which aspiring writers could display their forensic skill. Only those by Xenophon and Plato survive.) Xenophon shows Socrates in conversation with both fellow citizens and visitors to the city—sophists, generals, managers of large estates, young men with political ambitions. Their conversations address questions about how to live the best life with Socrates often offering practical advice as well as moral guidance. He tells brothers how to reconcile their quarrels and husbands how to educate their wives. In one memorable exchange on the latter topic, a friend asks Socrates how he can advise others when his own wife is notoriously difficult. He replies that if he has learned to deal with Xanthippe, he has met the toughest challenge a husband can face. The interests of Xenophon's Socrates extend beyond domestic and civic matters. Our Victorian translator offers this characterization of Book III, Chapter XI: "Discourse of Socrates with Theodota, an Athenian lady of no good character; wherein he endeavoureth in the most artful and engaging manner, to win her over from the criminal pleasures to which she was addicted unto the sublimer and more innocent delights of philosophy and virtue." The contemporary reader will be struck by the ambiguity of this flirtatious exchange.

Preview of MEMORABLE THOUGHTS OF SOCRATES

Perhaps the strangest picture of Socrates emerges in Xenophon's "Symposium." The contrast with Plato's work of the same name is striking. In Plato's masterpiece, a group of friends celebrate the divine Eros and the importance of erotic love in human life, especially pederastic love between older and younger men. Socrates somewhat undercuts this theme by claiming that everything he knows about love he learned from the priestess Diotima. He offers a long speech in her voice that has resonated over the centuries. The drinking party is interrupted by a drunken Alcibiades who offers a passionate and bitter portrait of Socrates from a rejected lover. Xenophon's banquet is less well known, but it offers special pleasures. The men's speeches range more widely, but erotic love is also center stage. The party's host is celebrating his friend Autolycus who has just won a wrestling contest, but the young man's father is present too (as chaperone?). Professional dancers have been invited to display their skills; eventually a young man and woman enact the love affair of Dionysus and Ariadne. The piece ends with the married men rushing home to their wives and the bachelors deciding they must marry soon. Perhaps the most memorable moment occurs after an initial solo performance by the young man. Socrates comments that dancing provides excellent exercise; he would like to learn the steps. Despite general laughter, one of the other guests confirms that one morning he caught the philosopher "in the act of dancing": "At first I stood aghast and feared me that you had parted with your senses." Nothing in Plato quite compares with this fleeting image. Imagine—a dancing Socrates!

Morris B. Kaplan
Professor of Philosophy
Purchase College SUNY